The New You
Lessons For Teen-age Girls

by Linda Wesbrooks

21ST CENTURY CHRISTIAN
PUBLICATIONS

2809 Granny White Pike
Nashville, Tennessee 37204

9th Printing
with content and book cover
revised and updated

ISBN 0-89098-406-9

CONTENTS

GUIDELINES FOR TEACHERS

Below is given the general outline of each chapter in this book. Although each lesson is different, each specific section of the chapters will always serve a certain purpose. Included with the outline of the book below are some suggestions on how to use each section of the chapter:

Discovery: In each lesson there is a *Discovery* section which examines an existing problem or condition facing most teen-age girls. This section will attempt to define and confine the particular subject being discussed. Also it will sometimes tell why the subject is important to young ladies.

The *Discovery* should always be read by teacher and student before class and discussed briefly in the classroom sessions. Try to get your students to relate to the problem or topic at hand—perhaps some of them may be dealing personally with the subject of the day. See that the girls understand how this topic is important to their lives...maybe some of them will volunteer to tell you how this subject concerns them.

What To Do: Of course, the *What To Do* section of each chapter attempts to solve the problem introduced in the *Discovery*. Practical hints and suggestions are presented which should help each girl deal with her individual needs. Notice that scripture is rarely quoted in this section, although all the suggestions are those that a Christian may follow. Correlated scriptures are given to be studied later in the chapter.

A Modern Parable: Next comes a short lesson in story form. Each modern parable presents a present-day situation involving the problem dealt with in that particular chapter. At the end of each parable is a moral, given in the style of an Aesop's fable. Some of the morals are serious; some are humorous; all contain an important idea.

Closing Thoughts: The *Closing Thoughts* section tries to summarize the main thoughts given in that chapter. Hopefully, this will make the outstanding ideas easier for the students to remember.

Thoughts For You: In this section questions are given for the pupils to answer before class. All answers should be written out so that in class a good discussion may ensue. Although only a few questions are given in each chapter, they're intended to stimulate rich ideas and class discussion. Take advantage of this section to get your girls to think, discuss, even debate.

Also a portion of scriptures connected with the lesson is given under *Thoughts For You*. These may be read beforehand and incorporated into the main discussion of the lesson. Be sure that time and careful study are given to the scriptures.

Lesson 1

Starting With Self: Personality

DISCOVERY

Your personality is your person-hood. It makes you distinct, individual—in short, it makes you be *you*. Already you have your own characteristics and traits which distinguish you from others about you. However, not many of us are completely satisfied with our personality. Often we sense that our personality is not attractive enough to others; that we need some improvement not only for our own sake but in order to make and keep new friends.

Perhaps a little self-examination will help you decide whether or not the present *you* is what you'd like to be. On the following chart, take a moment to look honestly at yourself and mark the things that are part of your personality. Am I...?

X talkative	X open-minded	X Christian
___ quiet	___ narrowminded	___ worldly
X outgoing	X respectful	X friendly
___ timid	___ insolent	___ aloof
X honest	___ bad tempered	___ snobbish
___ devious	X even tempered	X stubborn
___ quarrelsome	___ humble	___ easily led
X agreeable	___ proud	X organized
___ courageous	___ hard hearted	___ disheveled
___ frightened	X compassionate	___ messy

As you look at the things you marked, decide if this is the way you want to be. If not, get ready to make some changes.

WHAT TO DO?
Changing Your Personality

Changing your personality is a serious and awesome prospect. There are several things to keep in mind as you work on your personality—if you are in earnest about revising some part of *you*.

1. *Decide what characteristics need changing most.* Don't tackle a major overhaul at first—it's too difficult. Besides, not many of us are completely bad. Just pick out your most damaging characteristics and make up your mind to change things. Working on one trait at a time is probably the best way to progress.

2. Keep in mind that *the change you make must be genuine and gradual.* The you that has developed and existed for so many years cannot be changed overnight. A true change of part of your personality requires slow, patient, painstaking effort; any fast change is sure to be pretense.

A drastic, overnight change may cause you to lose the friends who liked you despite your former shortcoming. Think how shocked your friends would be if shy, quiet little you suddenly lambasted a party with jokes, laughter, and witty repertoire. Not only would you shock them, you would repel them. So effect your personality change gradually, making a genuine inner change as well as an outer one. A mere change of actions does not always indicate a true personality change.

3. *Select a good trait with which to replace the former one.* Otherwise, an even worse trait may overtake you. Like the man in Matthew 12:43 swept the unclean spirit from his heart, you may sweep all the bad characteristics from your life. Unless you fill that void with a desirable quality, however, evil things may come to inhabit your heart.

4. *Begin to think like the person you want to be.* Don't think like the old you, but like the new you. At first you will be conscious of your efforts—you'll have to remind yourself how to act occasionally. Yet soon, if you continue to think of yourself in the light of your new trait, that trait will become yours.

5. *Practice self-assurance.* It's important that you be self-assured in your efforts. Confident that the new you will be better than the old, don't be afraid to change.

At first, unobtrusively begin to practice your new trait, whatever it is. Go slowly and not too noticeably. Soon, if you add to your new quality gradually, everyone (including yourself) will hardly be aware of a change at all. Your new trait grew over a period of time, like all of your others. People *will* notice, however, that you are a much more interesting and attractive person than you formerly were.

A MODERN PARABLE

Ashley had often wondered why she was so lonely, but now it began to dawn on her: she had no friends! Well, there were plenty of boyfriends around, naturally, because Ashley was definitely the prettiest girl in school.

At that thought her eyebrows arched and a lilting smile flitted across her face. Yes, that's what everyone said—she was the beauty of the school.

"So why don't I have any girl friends?" she silently wailed. No girls ever chatted with her at her locker or asked her if she had her homework—or came around her, for that matter.

Suddenly, Ashley saw herself in her mind, walking down the hall at school. She was surrounded by boys, laughing sweetly, unaware of passing girls. In fact her nose was lifted a little bit into the air.

"I'm a snob!" She said it aloud, hit by a revelation. *"I am a snob!* No wonder the girls don't like me—why should they?" Determined, she began deeper self-examination. "Well, if I want any friends," she muttered, "I've got to try something."

Starting the next day, she smiled at some girls who passed her in the hallway. "Strange," she thought, "that I've never noticed them before." The day after that, she managed a "Hello" to some of them. Soon she found that she could converse and giggle with the other girls quite naturally.

Now Ashley was happy—happy that both girls and boys liked her better. And, what's more, she liked herself.

MORAL: *So if you don't like you, who will?*

CLOSING THOUGHTS

1. Your personality is distinctly you.
2. If changes need to be made, improve yourself genuinely and gradually.
3. Be steady—don't continually change your personality.
4. Build from within with confidence and your personality will truly be *you.*

THOUGHTS FOR YOU

1. QUESTIONS
   A. Define "personality" in your own words.

   B. What are some reasons you might have for changing parts of your personality?

C. Why is an overnight change in your actions unwise?

D. Write an honest appraisal of your own personality. Include both good and bad traits. Share these with the class and see if they agree with your self evaluation.

2. SCRIPTURES
    A. Personality traits you should possess
        1. Correct use of the tongue (Proverbs 15:1-4)
        2. Willingness to accept criticism (Proverbs 15:10;10:17; 9:8)
        3. Happiness or cheerfulness (Proverbs 15:13, 15)
        4. Respect for parents (Proverbs 15:20; Ephesians 6:1)
        5. Humility (Proverbs 16:5; 21:4)
        6. Compassion (Proverbs 19:17)
        7. Unbiased or unprejudiced view (Proverbs 28:21)
        8. Charity or love (1 Corinthians 13)

    B. Personality traits to develop (Titus 2:4-5)

3. SELF IMPROVEMENT. Below, list one trait of your personality you would like to change. Begin work on it today, but keep your decision secret for a while.

Lesson 2

Extending Yourself: Popularity

DISCOVERY

Popularity is synonymous with being well liked and accepted. No one feels self-sufficient enough to make it through life alone. Indeed, life would be practically meaningless without friends and a social life.

Why, then, is popularity sometimes regarded as something bad or worthy of scorn? Perhaps you've heard it said of someone, "All she wants is popularity," or "She's just doing that to be popular." Is popularity bad?

To find out, let's ask ourselves some preliminary questions. First of all, *popularity with whom?* This is an important decision that each individual must make. Remembering that being popular is being liked and accepted, you must realize that you cannot be liked and accepted by everyone. This is evident because people—their standards, their conduct, their likes and dislikes—are different.

Take, for example, the people you know. Perhaps you could divide them into several classifications:

(1) The Christian group. These people go to church services, have high moral standards, and refrain from improper types of entertainment.

(2) The middle group. In this group are relatively moral people—not Christians, but calm, steady folks. They may do a few things you don't approve of, but nothing drastic.

(3) The wild group. Anything from alcohol to drugs to weird entertainment is found in this group.

Now, from just a circle of your acquaintances, you can easily see that what would be popular with the first group of people would get you nowhere with the last group, or vice versa.

So, in deciding if popularity is bad, we might answer this: popularity with the wrong type of people is bad, if you must do wrong things to be popular with them. Popularity gained through doing right things is not bad.

Secondly, *how important is popularity to you?* If being popular is the foremost goal in your mind, this might become sin in your life. Perhaps you concentrate all your energies on charm, poise, and appearance to the extent that you neglect the inner qualities of personality that need to be developed. If this is true, then popularity is crowding out personality, and this is bad.

Keeping these ideas in mind, let's decide when popularity is right:
1. When you do right things and become popular, this is good.
2. When popularity does not take precedence over everything else in your life, this is good.
3. When development of Christian personality helps you gain popularity, this is good.

WHAT TO DO?
How To Be Popular

Popularity—being liked and accepted—is a two-way street. No one is ever liked unless he likes others. Therefore, a gain in popularity must correlate with a good personality. (You're still working on that from last week, aren't you?) Below is a list of some actions of personality that help your popularity. Check those that you feel you possess already. Work on the others.

___I try to smile or speak to everyone I know at school, church services and activities, etc.

___I try to smile or speak to strangers I pass at school, church services and activities, etc.

___I listen more than I talk in conversations.

___I am really interested in what others say.

___I look at the person with whom I am conversing.

___I try to look my best whenever I am seen in public.

___I know how to joke, laugh, and have a good time.

___I am subdued enough not to take over every party or conversation with my loud wit.

___I am outgoing enough to display my talents without shyness—say, singing or playing an instrument at a party.

___I try to speak to someone who looks timid or alone at parties or gatherings.

___I do not flirt with husbands or boyfriends of other girls.

___I do not embarrass others, even in the interest of laughter.

___I am not short, catty, or rude, even with someone I don't especially like.

___I don't use sarcasm often; and never at the expense of others.

___I ask sincerely about others who are sick and try to do something nice for them.

___I am considerate of older people, especially parents, as well as my own age group.

Needless to say, if you possess all of the above qualities, you are a popular person. The trick is simple but not easy: think of the other person—his needs, interests, and feelings—instead of yourself. If you do this, you will constantly find yourself assisting others, talking with them, helping them feel at ease—and you will be popular.

This is the reason Jesus was a popular man: He helped others, was genuinely concerned for them, and gave them primary consideration.

A MODERN PARABLE

Lauren slipped into her fabulous new dress and matching shoes. Parading before her full-length mirror, she was overcome by her own beauty. "Will I ever be a success tonight!" she thought. "With this new outfit and my new hair-do, I'll be the center attraction!"

Getting closer to the mirror, she scrutinized her make-up. Perfect. Flawless. Without a doubt, she would be the sensation of the party.

Arriving at Suzi's house a little late (so she could make an entrance) Lauren smiled with practiced charm. "Hello," she called in her best movie-star voice as she swished about the room. But, surprisingly, people only nodded and turned back to their companions to continue their conversation.

"I think we should take up a special collection for that orphanage," she overheard Bill say as she approached his group.

"Hi, Billy!" The studied smile flashed again.

Bill returned her greeting, then went on. "They are building a new dormitory, I hear, and need new furniture for the orphans."

Stunned and angry, Lauren headed for the CD player. Putting on the newest hit disc, she adjusted her marvelous dress and began to dance the newest wild dance.

"Hey, look at Lauren!" a boy cried.

At last, she thought. *My moment has come!*

Most people turned to look. A few of them laughed; others turned away in disgust. "Lauren sure is desperate," one girl commented.

Some boys surrounded Lauren, laughing and punching one another. When the disc ended, one boy whispered something in Lauren's ear that she didn't want to hear. The rest of the party ignored her and went on talking animatedly about their newest church project.

Exhausted from her dance and angry at the turn the night had taken, Lauren flounced away from the party, still looking absolutely flawless in her outfit. Outwardly flawless, that is.

MORAL: Do not mistake attention-getting for popularity; or, So who wants to be a sensation, anyway?

CLOSING THOUGHTS

1. Decide with whom you wish to be popular and act accordingly. Hopefully, you will choose Christian friends as your very closest associates.
2. Do not let popularity become the over-riding motive in all you do. If you do, you will be trying to be an attraction, not a truly popular person.
3. Popularity is earned. If you do not develop a genuine interest in others, any popularity you enjoy will be short-lived.
4. Let being popular with Christ be your foremost desire.
5. Remember that true popularity with the right people is good, since it requires a Christian personality development on your part.

THOUGHTS FOR YOU

1. QUESTIONS
   A. Give some reasons why being popular can be good.

   B. Give some reasons why being popular can be wrong or bad.

   C. Cite some examples (anonymously, of course) you have witnessed where people have tried to gain popularity by merely getting attention.

   D. Can you remain popular even if some of your ideas are unpopular? (Discuss or give examples.)

   E. Share with the class the personality trait you chose last week
   ·   to try to develop. See if they have noticed your efforts, have noticed an improvement, or if they think you haven't tried at all. Let the class decide if this personality change will contribute to your popularity.

2. SCRIPTURES
   CHRIST: popular with most of the common people.
   Luke 2:52
   Matthew 8:18
   John 6:2
   John 6:15

   CHRIST: unpopular with many important people. Many of His ideas were unpopular.
   Mark 12:12-13
   Mark 14:1
   John 8:59
   John 6:60
   John 6:66

   CHRISTIAN: may be unpopular with evil or non-Christian people.
   John 15:18-19
   1 Peter 4:16
   2 Timothy 3:12
   Luke 6:26

   GOD'S PEOPLE: Some who were popular for good works.
   Esther 2:15-17
   Genesis 39:21; 41:14-43
   Daniel 1:9

But these people, too, had their unpopular moments with certain people.

3. SELF IMPROVEMENT: Continue to work on the personality trait you have chosen to develop. See if this improvement adds to your popularity.

Lesson 3

Beyond Yourself: Parents

DISCOVERY

Parents are some of the most misunderstood people in the world. They are condemned, shouted at, and accused by their children and by those who blame all of the world's problems on the older generation.

Too often, young people forget that their parents are very similar to them—merely older and more experienced, but still like them. It is not enough to shout that parents are not experienced, that they have only repeated annually their past mistakes. Neither is it adequate to blame all our problems and frustrations on them, to accuse them of not understanding teen-agers, to scorn them as "out of it" and "old-fashioned."

Not only are many of these things untrue, but such talk only widens the gap between parent and teen rather than uniting the family. So before you write your parents off as a lost cause, take a little test to see what kind of standing *you* have with your parents. See how far you've gone to pave the road toward good family relations:

___Do you try to understand your parents' point of view as well as expect them to understand yours?

___Are you aware that your parents are sensitive and that angry, caustic words can hurt their feelings and cause them heartache?

___Do you realize that most parents act with your good in mind?

___Would you really be happy if your parents weren't old-fashioned—if they competed in your age group for the attention of your friends?

___When a disagreement arises, do you sit down to reason with your parents rather than sling tearful accusations at them which have little to do with the issue at hand?

___Do you bother to communicate or associate with your parents at times other than when you want or need something from them?

By your answers, perhaps you can get a picture of yourself in regard to your parents. Is your side of things less than desirable? If your relationship with your parents lacks something, at least *you* can take action to improve things.

WHAT TO DO?
Getting Along With Parents

Before you can be good friends with your parents, you must cultivate some proper attitudes. First, let's examine what *should* your attitude toward your parents be?

First of all, you owe your parents *respect*. Their age and position of authority over you require it. As you yourself can attest, nothing is more sickening than a pert, sarcastic youth who continually cuts down, slanders and "smarts off" with his parents in public or in private.

Secondly, you owe them *gratitude*. Since you were born, you have depended upon your parents in countless ways. You have been able to take for granted the food on the table, the clothes you wear, the cosmetics you use, the house you live in. Of course—these are material things. But you couldn't live without most of them. Too, your parents—if they are Christians—have tried to supply moral standards and a religious background to see you through life.

Thirdly, you owe your parents *understanding*. Too often, young people cry, "My parents don't understand me!" Do you try to understand *them*? You'll never completely understand them, or yourself for that matter, but if the effort is to be made, you should not shove all the responsibility onto your parents.

So since you and your parents must live and work together, why not try to make these years happy? The years at home are all too few, as everyone later discovers, and a bickering, unhappy home life is unnecessary and will someday be regretted.

Now that you understand better the attitudes and feelings you should have for your parents, below are some common problems that arise between parent and teen and some suggestions for solving those problems. Reading and following these ideas should help make yours a better home life in relation to your parents.

1. First of all, *your personality may sometimes clash with your parents'*, as well as with anyone you know. In order that this not be a major catastrophe, parents and off-spring should keep this in mind: all personalities are different, but if all personalities strive to be Christlike, clashes will diminish.

2. Secondly, *problems may often arise with your parents because of your neglected home life.* Perhaps you resent your parents' unwillingness to let you go places as often as you would like. Could it be because you are shirking your home duties and your folks want you

at home to help out? Wake up, girls! Volunteer for the morning dishes, and maybe Mom will do the dinner clean-up, leaving you free to go out. Don't let your mother ask you more than once to empty the trash or vacuum the floors. Not only is it easier to do all of your tasks, *then* relax or go out—it makes for less arguing and nagging around the house. Keep your room clean and neat—your parents will be impressed with your sense of responsibility. A responsible girl should be allowed to go out more often; logical, isn't it?

3. Thirdly, *the question of authority may arise.* Often teen-agers dislike the rules and orders given to them by parents. Keep in mind, however, that this is a God-given task and your parents are over you as long as you live under their roof. It is also a law of the land that juveniles are under their parents' jurisdiction. For example, most states require your parents to sign you away if you wish to marry before the age of twenty-one.

If you feel that your parents are too strict, ask yourself why. Does it go back to your sloppy or irresponsible home life—do they feel that you are not self-disciplined? If this is so, practice bossing yourself around. Make yourself toe the line and be more mature. Undoubtedly the strictness of your parents will let up.

If you think that you are doing nothing to make your parents question your maturity and judgment, sit down and have an honest talk (not argument) with them. In all likelihood, they are afraid for you and hesitate to cut the apron strings. Perhaps their parents were very strict with them and this causes them to carry on similar dealings with you.

Show them you will be worthy of their trust. Work out a sensible curfew with them; tell them if you ever violate it you will go back under their old severe rules. Tell them you will introduce them to all of your dates before you go out. In short, re-assure them and build up their confidence in you—then never betray that confidence!

4. Finally, *never let the problem of friend versus family arise.* If your friends cannot respect and abide by the guidelines your family sets for you, you need to trade in your friends. Anyone who cannot respect parents, who jeers at the "old man," who violates the trust his family puts in him, is certainly a despicable person with whom to associate.

It is hoped that by following the suggestions given in this chapter that your relationship with your parents will become much more satisfactory because *you* made that special effort.

A MODERN PARABLE

"Aw, John, yer parents'll never know!" It was Billy, always the loudmouth and ring-leader, offering John the can of beer.

A chorus of "Yeah, mama's boy" arose from the other four boys in the car.

As John eyed the beer warily, he was aware of the sneers and jibes of the fellows. He also heard the echo of his mother's words whenever he left the house. "Be a good boy, John, like your father would want you to be." Biting his lip, he thought of his father—dead now for two years—and the Christian life he had led.

"Aw, his mama might spank him," taunted Billy. "We don't want Johnnie to get a spankin'!"

Fiercely John grabbed Billy's wrist and beer sloshed out of the can onto his shirt. The boys laughed as he held the can, staring at it while a terrific inner battle took place. He hated for his mother to call him a boy—but that's what she always said: "Be a good boy." Eyeing the beer can, he wondered, "Will *this* make me a man?"

"It ain't *holding* it that helps," laughed Billy. "It's *drinkin'* it."

Suddenly something inside was burning. Glancing at his watch, John saw that the 12:00 o'clock town curfew would soon be in effect. He looked around, too, at the distorted, half-drunken faces that were beside him. The smell of the beer nauseated him.

"Let me out of here," he growled, shoving open the back door and climbing over another fellow to get out.

"But we ain't killed this case of beer yet!"

"Don't ya know Johnnie's gotta be home at midnight," laughed another boy, punching his buddy. "Or he'll turn into a pumpkin!"

Their laughter followed John as he strode along the street toward home. A light breeze blew in his face and every breath invigorated him. Inside, the warm feeling began to spread.

MORAL: Following Christian parental guidance not only makes you feel right—it is right.

CLOSING THOUGHTS

1. Parents are people with feelings and emotions, just like you.
2. Develop the proper attitude toward your parents and an improvement in family relations is sure to occur.
3. Give your parents consideration and they will return the favor.
4. Show your maturity and responsibility in your home life and your parents will feel that you are worthy of trust and responsibility in all areas of life.

20

THOUGHTS FOR YOU

1. QUESTIONS
   A. Interview a classmate or acquaintance and get his three major problems or complaints about parents.

   B. Interview the parents of the teen you interviewed and find out their three major problems or complaints about teen-agers.

   C. Using the facts you gathered above (you might conduct the interviews simultaneously), list three steps that family (or any family with those problems) might take to improve family relations. (The family should be kept anonymous.)

2. SCRIPTURES
   Responsibility of off-spring toward parents.
   Matthew 15:1-9
   Ephesians 6:1-3
   Colossians 3:20
   Proverbs 1:8; 4:1; 10:1; 23:22

   Responsibility of parents toward off-spring.
   Genesis 18:19
   Deuteronomy 6:3-9
   Proverbs 22:6
   Ephesians 6:4

3. Your personality and popularity cannot be complete without a good relationship with your parents. Try especially this week to be courteous, helpful, and understanding toward them. Everyone's life will then be happier and more peaceful.

Lesson 4

The School Situation: Friends and Extra-Curricular Activities

DISCOVERY

Having the friendship of others is akin to popularity, but really goes much deeper. A true friend holds *love* for you rather than merely liking you.

Since everyone is required to attend school for twelve years, the making and keeping of friends becomes a major project—and perhaps a major problem. Everyone has experienced at some time the feeling of loneliness, of being left out. As a child, you may have played alone on the playground. In junior high school, you may have been unattractive and, since you felt undesirable, you shied away from the group. Even in high school—where the choice of friends is wide and varied—you may at times find yourself feeling very much unwanted and alone.

On Saturday night, you feel that everyone has a date but you. At the ballgame, your best friend Krista sits with her boyfriend and you would feel awkward sitting with them; so you don't. In P.E. class, you're not very good at basketball so you're chosen last when the captains pick their teams.

And how do you react to this? In most instances, you pretend not to care. You try to shrug it off and pretend that it doesn't matter at all, when really it does.

But now is the time to face facts. Now is the time to quit pretending and admit certain things to yourself. See if you can really believe the statements below. Read them carefully and digest them. Check those you sincerely agree with:

___School is a miniature society; it contains its share of successes and failures.

___To want and need close friends is natural.

___Feeling left out and unwanted is an emotion that comes to all at one time or another—even the most popular people you know.

___Being alone at some social gatherings is not necessarily bad— as long as you don't feel uncomfortable about it.

___Feeling left out may mean that you are unsure of yourself and your ability to mingle and mix with people.

___Sometimes friendship is a crutch—something to hold onto in case all else goes bad.

___At times friends are jealous because another friend begins to date.

___If you often feel left out, you should become more involved and put more effort into being a part of things.

WHAT TO DO?
Being Part of the School Situation

Getting involved in school activities is good for many reasons. One of them is that you form more friendships and begin to associate at ease with many people. If one of your problems is that you are not a part of things or don't have enough true friends, this chapter is designed to help you.

First of all, realize that few people are naturally in great demand for friendship, for clubs, for activities. You are not indispensable, in other words, so the effort must be made by you. Most high school clubs can be joined voluntarily—so, all you must do is make yourself available to them. Then the real work begins. Be useful in your organization—go to meetings, to the annual party; volunteer for the after-school work. What better way to meet and learn to work with more friends?

Secondly, don't drop all of your old friends. It is important to branch out, to not confine yourself, because you want to be at ease wherever you are. You'd like to guarantee that you could find a friend at any party, someone to sit with at any ballgame. But don't just exchange one set of friends for another. Instead, keep all your old friends and your new. Be likeable and flexible so that you can fit in wherever you are.

Thirdly, keep a best friend, but don't be naive. At this time of your life, you desire a best friend to whom you tell your secrets, confide your hopes, and with whom you go many places. If you do not confine yourself to the friend exclusively, then a best friend is great!

But do not leave yourself open for hurt. Be aware that a best friend will probably begin to date (or you will) a special boy. This will not terminate your friendship, but it will change things. Your friend will concentrate on her sweetheart more than on you; she will desire his company above yours; she will share her time with him rather than with you. Realizing how natural this is, you must not let petty jealousy result. Too, if your extra-curricular activities have let you find and form new friendships, you will have other associates rather than be completely alone.

24

Fourthly, do not let the up-sweep of increased social activity put you in a bad position. Being in many clubs and organizations, you will find yourself busy; sought after. It is possible, however, that many activities in which your new friends and acquaintances engage do not suit your Christian ideals. Getting involved with new companions does not mean you must compromise your beliefs. In fact, should you ever have to choose, your beliefs are far more important.

But will you have to give up your new friends? Probably not. You may have to by-pass a few activities and stay away from certain situations, but this does not mean you have lost your friends.

For example, there is nothing wrong with being a cheerleader. But suppose some things of which you do not approve have been occurring on the bus which the cheerleaders and football players ride to and from the games. Does this mean you must not be a cheerleader? Certainly not. But you may have to be a different cheerleader, letting it be known that you do not intend to participate in anything wrong.

Finally, do not let friends and extra-curriculars interfere with your home and church activities. Allot time for all of them and you will be a well-rounded individual.

When Friendship Fails

Often, friendships are terminated because of silly misunderstandings or false information. Still more often, friendships die because one or both parties have had bad feelings for the other as a result of any number of things. Many teens ask: "How can I keep my friends?" Below are some suggestions for keeping friends. If you need improvement in a certain area, put an X beside it and resolve to change.

___Never, *never* gossip about anyone—friend or foe.

___Do not divulge to others something that a friend told you in secret.

___Do not repeat unpleasant information about anyone—even if it is true.

___Do not be jealous of a friend's friendship with others—whether boys or girls.

___Never try to steal a friend's boyfriend, even if they are not "steadies."

___Be a true friend even if one of your friends is not popular with the "in" crowd.

___Do not choose as friends only those to whom you feel superior in some way.

___Don't be a "fair-weather" friend.

A MODERN PARABLE

Cherie sat proudly by David's side on the way home from their date. For as long as she could remember, she had wanted to go with David Sutton.

Chattering ceaselessly about their friends, she soon brought up the names of Debbie Stanton and Kyle Barton, two of her good friends. She noticed that David perked up with interest when she mentioned their names, the remembered that he and Kyle were close friends.

"Say," said David, "you and Debbie are practically best friends. How does she really feel about Kyle?"

"Well, just between you and me," Cherie lowered her voice confidentially, "Debbie and I were talking about that just the other day. You know, she really doesn't care that much for Kyle—although she thinks he's a great guy. She still cares for her old boyfriend. Said she'd take him back in a snap if he'd only ask her."

"She would, would she?" David's eyes were gleaming, but Cherie failed to notice and continued her chatter.

Monday at school Cherie hummed a little tune as she walked down the hall, until she was accosted by Debbie. "Hi, Deb!"

"Hi, indeed!" Sparks of anger flew from her friend's eyes. "What have you been saying about me? Kyle will hardly speak to me, and when I get to the bottom of it all—it's *you*, my supposed friend!"

Saturday night's careless conversation re-echoed in her ears and Cherie's face burned. So David had told Kyle! "Please, Debbie. I told David all of that in confidence!"

"Well, when Kyle's speaking to me again, I might consider speaking to you!" cried Debbie hotly. "And thanks a lot."

MORAL: A friend sticketh closer than a boyfriend.

CLOSING THOUGHTS

1. To avoid being left out, get involved in extra-curricular activities at school.
2. Make new friends, keep old friends, and do not compromise your standards for any of your friends.
3. Once you have made friends, you must make an effort to keep them.

THOUGHTS FOR YOU

1. QUESTIONS
   A. Discuss the obligations put upon you by friendship.

   B. What are some things that even friendship does not require of you? (*i.e.,* What would you *not* do for a friend?)

   C. Everyone has at one time lost a friend or at least quarreled with one. Recount your experience. What caused the trouble between you and your friend? What could've prevented it?

2. SCRIPTURES
   Being friends with God.
   James 2:23
   John 15:13-16
   Proverbs 18:24

   Friends on earth.
   Betrayed friendship.
   Proverbs 6:2-3
   Micah 7:5
   Luke 21:16

   True friendship.
   Proverbs 17:17
   Proverbs 18:24
   Proverbs 27:9-10

3. Is your relationship with your parents improving? Continue to work on last week's reminder to be more courteous and understanding. Soon it will come naturally.

Lesson 5

The School Situation: Teachers and Studies

DISCOVERY

Teachers seem to be a special breed of people. To students, they sometimes appear ruthless slave-drivers, determined to while away all of their pupils' leisure time with endless homework. However, teachers serve a useful and important purpose—in fact, one of the most important in the world. To them are entrusted the minds of the young: minds which must learn skills, techniques, and knowledge that will aid them throughout life.

If your attitude toward your teachers is that of distrust and dislike, consider the picture from the teacher's point of view: There he is, facing anywhere from twenty to fifty lively, talkative, energetic students. When he demands quiet, it is rarely given. When he assigns homework to help you learn, perhaps four people out of forty do as they are asked. No one volunteers to answer the questions he asks to stimulate discussions. Constantly someone is misbehaving or playing pranks, making it impossible for him to teach or others to learn. To top it all, he spent a fortune on his education (and must continue to go to school periodically throughout his teaching career) yet is one of the most underpaid of all professionals in many states.

Does that sound like an easy life? The fact is, most teachers are nice people who are often forced to the defensive and into the role of harsh disciplinarian because of the actions of some of their students. Of course, not all teachers are great, or sincere, for that matter—but neither are all students.

So what is the problem? It's how to get along with teachers—not teachers as a group, but teachers as individuals.

Secondly, perhaps your relationship with teachers, your lack of study, or your difficulty in learning make your studies in school very hard. Perhaps that "C" should have been a "B." So another problem that school presents is its study courses. How do you study? Can you learn without memorizing? Several questions concerning your studies will be dealt with in this chapter.

WHAT TO DO?
Teachers and Studies

To begin with, your relationship with most teachers should and can be good. Occasionally a personality conflict prevents your being best friends, but there are ways to avoid antagonizing teachers.

Below are some attitude and action suggestions which should bring results in your efforts to understand and adapt to your teachers. Check those suggestions you already follow. Work toward the others.

___Realize the momentous task your teacher faces, and the problems brought about by this task.

___Look at each teacher as a person, just like yourself—not a citizen from another planet.

___Understand that classroom co-operation will stand you in good stead with any teacher.

___Even though you do not always agree with what your teacher is saying, listen politely. Disparaging facial expressions are just as bad as disparaging remarks.

___Disagree in a respectful manner. When a teacher needs correcting, do so in a helpful manner.

___Follow your teacher's instructions.

___Listen and do not ask unnecessary questions. It is irritating to a teacher to have to repeat instructions for a day-dreaming student.

___Talk to your teachers as a friend before and after class, but do not monopolize their time. Get to know them as real people.

___Do something nice for your teachers occasionally, but don't try to butter them up.

___Do not avoid your teachers in the halls or in the community as if they had the plague. Speak to them wherever you see them.

Most teachers are willing to be friendly and helpful. As stated before, many students put teachers on the defensive, thus meriting the teachers' disapproval. If you've ever wondered what actions a teacher despises, read the list below and avoid these troublesome characteristics.

A teacher disapproves of:

(1) A student who must repeatedly be told to discontinue some action, or to *do* a particular thing.

(2) Students who talk or otherwise interrupt while the teacher is talking.

(3) Students who do not listen.

(4) Students who work on their homework for English during their Physics class.

(5) Students who make "cute" or sarcastic remarks either to or about the teacher.

(6) Students who try to distract those who are trying to learn.

(7) Students who do any of the above, then deny doing it.

If any of the above fit you, your popularity with teachers may be low. The teachers may not dislike *you*, but they will dislike your actions and constantly be irritated with *you*—because you are responsible for your actions. Besides, teachers are human, and how many people can separate their abhorrence for someone's actions from the person doing those actions? If you want your teachers to like and approve of you, make sure they like and approve of your actions.

Perhaps other problems plague you, however. Are you an average student who feels that teachers are partial to the brighter students? That may be true. But probably the teachers are, again, associating a pupil's actions with the pupil himself.

Most bright students are well behaved. If you want more teacher approval and popularity, pattern your behavior after that of a bright student. This will also help improve your grades:

1. *Bright students listen.* By listening, they learn what the teachers want them to know. Because they listen—teachers like them. Because they listen—their grades are good.

2. *Bright students do their homework.* Because of this—teachers like them. Because of this—they learn and their grades are good.

3. *Bright students respect the teacher.* They recognize his superior knowledge and ability. Because of this—teachers like them. Because of this—they try harder and their grades are good.

Finally comes the problem of study. Maybe you have good relationships with your teachers, but your grades could stand improvement.

First of all, how do you study? Each person must develop his own techniques over a period of time. Usually study of facts (math formulas, history dates) does involve memorization—committing certain things to memory. A study of a literary work, a philosophy, or anything involving a mass of thoughts and facts usually requires a general knowledge or concept of the thoughts—an understanding of them. This will *not* entail unyielding memorization.

Below are some hints for helpful study. These would work also for Sunday School study:

1. Gather your materials. Make sure that rulers, compasses, pencils, and paper are all present so you will not have to jump up to find something.

2. Select an appropriate place. Usually this means somewhere where others will not be present. Have good lighting, and a table or desk on which to work. If the radio helps rather than hinders your study, turn it on.

3. Get in the right frame of mind. Resolve that you will study—not day-dream, not talk to Michelle on the telephone.

4. Review your previous studies. Look over the notes from last week. See how the things you learned prior to now fit in with your studies for today. Once you refresh your mind and get your knowledge in perspective, learning will come naturally.

5. See things in sequence. Make your mind grasp that you are studying Dwight Eisenhower after Harry Truman because of the sequence of their places in history.

6. Use substitute memorization to learn long lists. Learn the first letter of each word, or the first word of each sentence. Then associate that letter or word with what you must know. For example, if learning a list of poets: Hawthorne, Holmes, Longfellow, Lowell, Poe, and Whittier—memorize HHLLPW. Then you will remember the names.

7. Learn by association. Funny or trick association will often work. An example from Bible Study are the words Sadducees and Pharisees. How do you recall which group didn't believe in the resurrection? It was the *Sad*ducees—isn't it *sad* that they had no hope?

8. Repeat (aloud if possible) several times what you have learned. Only by repetition will the facts remain in mind.

9. Review for a moment just before class. While everyone else is babbling, or while the teacher calls the roll, you can get one last refresher.

10. Be sure to ask the teacher about anything you do not understand in advance of the test. Do not wait until he passes a test paper to you to ask the question that has been on your mind for days.

A MODERN PARABLE

Jennifer rushed to class and stepped inside the door moments after the bell had rung. "Jennifer," her teacher remarked, "that's the third time you've been late this week."

Sulkily, Jennifer walked to her desk. After class she told Sheila, "That ole teacher. All she does is fuss. Didn't she look awful in that yellow suit she wore today?"

"Why are you always late, anyway?" Sheila stopped at her locker.

"Well...Brad and I have to see one another between classes. And by the time I talk to him, I'm late!"

"Then why blame Mrs. Ellis?" They started toward the library. "There *is* a school rule against being tardy."

32

"Sheila!" Jennifer turned wide eyes to her best friend. "Are you going to side with a teacher against *me*?"

Sheila shrugged. "I just think you're lucky. She could've sent you to the office every day you've been late and you would've been in detention by now."

Jennifer thought for a long moment. Then, "I guess Mrs. Ellis has been pretty tolerant, hasn't she?" she murmured. "Maybe from now on I can be on time."

MORAL: Blaming others for your own faults is a bad reflection on you know who.

CLOSING THOUGHTS

1. Realize the personhood of your teachers.
2. Make an effort to be friendly with your teachers.
3. If your teachers like your actions, they will probably like you. If they disapprove of your actions, it will be difficult for them to like you.
4. Your studies can be easier if you prepare to study, spend time at it, and review several times.

THOUGHTS FOR YOU

1. QUESTIONS
   A. Think of your favorite teacher, one you like who approves of you. Describe your behavior around this particular teacher—both in and out of the classroom.

   B. If a certain teacher seems to disapprove of you, describe your behavior toward this teacher—in and out of the classroom.

   C. Compare your answers to the two questions above. Below write some suggestions that you might follow in order to be more popular with the teacher in question B.

D. What is your greatest problem in studying? Write it below and let the class make suggestions that might help you overcome this problem.

2. SCRIPTURES
   Respect for authority, experience, knowledge
   Proverbs 1:5
   Proverbs 4:20
   Proverbs 5:12-13
   Proverbs 12:15
   Proverbs 10:20

   Diligence in learning and personal discipline in study
   Proverbs 4:7, 13
   Proverbs 8:33
   Proverbs 12:1
   Proverbs 16:23
   Proverbs 21:11
   Proverbs 23:12, 23

   Heed and study God's Word
   Proverbs 1:25
   Proverbs 15:28
   1 Thessalonians 4:11
   2 Timothy 1:13
   2 Timothy 2:15
   2 Timothy 3:16

3. Begin now to make special efforts to be a model student for both public and Sunday School teachers.

Lesson 6

Concerning Your Career

DISCOVERY

Choosing and pursuing a career are two of the major steps in your life. Although some women do not pursue their career throughout life, it is still an important choice. Even if you do not plan to work once you are married, you will probably work for several years after you finish your education, spending money on clothes, saving for your wedding and trousseau, contributing your offering to the church. Too, many women—in this world of high prices—find it necessary to keep their vocation after marriage at least until their children are born, and later go back to work after the children are grown.

So, even if you plan to marry immediately after you finish your education, do not lightly brush aside the subject of a career. Perhaps you will find it necessary to work for a living someday.

Choosing a career can be a problem; so can pursuing that career. After you have decided the type of work you prefer and the type of training you need, you must find a place of business that will hire you.

Realizing the problems involved in vocation selecting and securing, this chapter will devote itself to some primary questions: Why should I train for a career I might never use? How do I select my line of work and training? How do I go about getting a job?

WHAT TO DO?
Pursuing Your Career

First of all, many girls neglect to plan for a career because they contend that they will marry quickly and depend on their husbands for support. Although the number of girls who feel this way is diminishing, there are still those left who learn no training or skills which might later benefit them in a job.

So, below are listed several reasons which, it is hoped, will convince girls that they should be *prepared* to work—regardless of whether or not they *plan* to work:

1. You may never marry, or may not marry for several more years. In either case, you must work for your living.

2. You may marry a man who needs some years of advancement in his work before he is able to support the both of you. You would be required to work.

3. You may marry, become bored as a housewife, and want to work.

4. You may marry, and after a period of time, determine that your husband is unfaithful to you, leading to divorce and the need for you to work to support yourself.

5. Your husband may die or become disabled. You would find it necessary to support yourself and perhaps an ailing mate.

In spite of the feeling among some that women should never work, it sometimes becomes imperative that they do so—even wives and mothers. Do not leave this void in your life so that you would be helpless if you ever needed to find a job.

Since the necessity of preparing for a career has been established, the question next arises: "What career should I choose?" Below are some helpful guidelines in selecting the line of work you might like:

1. If you like to work with children and young people, you might be:

a teacher	a teacher (tutoring, music, etc)
a child psychologist	a social worker
a speech therapist	a welfare employee
a physical therapist	a worker with an adoption agency

2. If you feel the desire to be of service to all people, regardless of age, you might be:

a teacher	a dental assistant
a nurse	a dentist
a doctor	a librarian
a receptionist	a customer service representative

3. If you are orderly and efficient and enjoy being with people your own age, you might be:

a legal assistant	a data entry employee
an editor	a bookkeeper
a computer programmer	a lab technician
an accountant	an engineer

Some other considerations:

1. If you plan to marry soon after finishing high school, or if you do not plan to attend college, it will be best to choose a career for which

you can train in high school. Girls in this category would take typing, computer, and accounting courses—as many as were available—and be ready to take on a job after graduation. In some high schools, other vocational or co-op courses may be offered.

2. If no immediate marriage plans are ahead for you, you will be freer to choose a career which requires special training or a college degree. Choose wisely, however. Do not begin training for a career—wasting time, energy, money—if you feel you might not finish your training.

3. If you plan to work for several years, even after marriage, then it will be feasible for you to go to college. If you plan only to work if you must, then swift, efficient business study courses would be in order for you. Secretaries, word processors, clerks, are always in demand.

4. Choose something that interests you. A job is a weekly proposition which can be frustrating and boring if you do not enjoy your work. According to your interests and future plans, you should be able to select a job well-suited for you.

Suppose you have decided what type of work you would like to do and have completed your training for it; or perhaps you are prepared for summer employment which will help you pay for the training ahead. Now comes the moment of realization: you go in search of a job.

Many people worry and wonder about how to go about getting a job. Although procedures differ with each place of business, there are several things to keep in mind that will help you as you search for employment. Study the following outline carefully. Hopefully, it will answer many questions you may have about finding a job.

I. When to apply for a job.
   A. Summer work.
      1. Six months ahead of the time you want to work, you should apply.
      2. Summer work is in great demand by both high school and college students.
      3. Get your application in early so you will be considered first.
   B. Permanent work.
      1. Applying early is still the rule.
      2. As soon as you decide where you might like to work, apply there.
         a. Employers often cannot hire you immediately, but an early application assures them of your interest in the job.
         b. Usually the earliest applications are considered first.

C. Time of day to apply.
  1. Begin early.
  2. If you go to several places of business, try to visit them all before lunch.
    a. By applying for jobs in the morning, you let prospective employers know you are eager and interested.
    b. In the morning, both you and the employer are fresh and feeling your best.
  3. Do not try to beat the company employees to work. Arrive early, but not that early.

II. Approaching the company.
  A. The oral approach.
    1. You may go in person to a place of business and fill out an application for a job.
    2. Since this is done without an appointment, you may find it impossible to obtain an interview that day.
  B. The written approach.
    1. Some companies desire a written letter of application.
    2. In this letter you would list your qualifications, tell why you would like to have the job, and request an interview at the employer's convenience.
      a. Your address and telephone number should be included.
      b. You should not go to the company until you receive a response to your letter.
  C. The telephone approach.
    1. It is usually wise to call ahead—if only to make certain that the company is interviewing prospective workers on that day.
    2. You should request the personnel office and politely ask to set up an interview date.
      a. Be sure to write down the exact time and place of the interview.
      b. Many times you will be told to come in at your convenience—or perhaps be given a day to come in when other applicants will also be there.

III. Whom to see.
  A. At any place of business you will be met by a secretary or receptionist.
    1. He or she may administer tests and give you an application form to complete.
    2. However, the secretary does not do the company's hiring and firing.

B. You must see the personnel manager or someone from the personnel office to be interviewed for the job.
   1. Take all tests carefully but swiftly, since you will be timed.
   2. After completing tests and your application form, ask to see the personnel manager for an interview. If you have an appointment, be sure to say so.

IV. Filling out the application form.
  A. Although the interview is most important, it is also important that you leave a neat, accurate representative of yourself behind. That is your application.
    1. It should be filled out neatly.
    2. It will have instructions to follow: follow them and give all requested information.
    3. You should *print* all information unless otherwise instructed.
  B. Information called for.
    1. On the next page is a sample application form.
    2. Questions vary with each firm.
      a. Be truthful in answering all questions.
      b. List as references a minister, a businessman, a former teacher or principal, unless otherwise instructed.

V. The interview.
  A. The interviewer's job is to find out about you, what you can do, and if you will be a reliable worker.
  B. What the interviewer may ask.
    1. About former jobs and skills you possess.
    2. About school grades and interests.
  C. What the interviewer will tell you.
    1. How you did on your performance tests.
    2. What jobs are available.
    3. Whether or not you have a chance of being hired.
    4. When you will know if you got the job.
  D. Your part of the interview.
    1. Appearance
      a. Be neat.
      b. Be clean.
      c. Be businesslike.
    2. Attitude.
      a. Smart-alecks don't have a chance.
      b. An adult, responsible position requires an adult, responsible attitude.
      c. Have quiet self-confidence, but don't be a braggart.

NAME _____
          (LAST)   (FIRST)   (MIDDLE)

SEX (M)__ (F)__
MARITAL STATUS:
SINGLE__ MARRIED__ WIDOWED__ DIVORCED__

ADDRESS _____ TELEPHONE _____
         (STREET) (CITY/STATE) (ZIP)

NAME OF PARENT, GUARDIAN OR MATE _____

HAVE YOU EVER BEEN ARRESTED? _____
WHY?_____

SERVED IN ARMED SERVICES ____ WHICH BRANCH? _____
HONORABLY DISCHARGED? _____

EDUCATION (CIRCLE LAST YEAR OF SCHOOL COMPLETED)
1 2 3 4 5 6 7 8 9 10 11 12 13 14 15 16 17 18 19 20

SKILLS OF WHICH YOU ARE CAPABLE _____
_____

TYPE OF JOB IN WHICH YOU ARE INTERESTED _____
DAYS AND HOURS YOU ARE WILLING TO WORK _____
EXPECTED SALARY: _____

FORMER PLACES OF EMPLOYMENT: LIST EMPLOYER NAME
AND ADDRESS AND DATES OF EMPLOYMENT

_____

_____

_____

REFERENCES: (THREE WITH ADDRESSES & PHONE NUMBERS).

1._____

2._____

3._____

d. Answer all questions truthfully and sincerely; do not make light of them.
3. Conversation.
   a. Have a respectful tone of voice.
   b. Say something only when you understand what you're saying.
   c. Pause to think if necessary.
   d. Let the employer do the interviewing.

A MODERN PARABLE

Megan took the tests back to the receptionist's desk and watched while her answers were graded. "You passed everything—and made excellent in math," the lady smiled.

"Great!" said Megan, relief flooding her. "Now could I talk with the personnel manager?"

"Dear, he's busy right now," the receptionist answered, still smiling. "Besides, we're not doing any hiring right now. Why don't you come back in a few weeks, hmmm?"

"Well..." Megan left, downhearted. Getting a job seemed to be an impossible task. Down the hot sidewalk she went, wondering if she would ever find work.

Then a sudden determination swept her. "If they aren't hiring," she thought, "why did they give me those tests?" Resolutely she turned and headed back for the company she had just left.

"Hello again," she told the surprised receptionist, seating herself in the lobby. "I know the personnel manager is busy, but I think I'll wait until he's free to interview me. That way he'll at least keep me in mind if a job comes up. That is—if it's all right..."

"Of course, dear." The smile was still on her face—a bit icy, perhaps, but still there. "I'll tell Mr. Rogers you're here."

MORAL: Even if the early bird has to eat a few worms, she may still get the job.

CLOSING THOUGHTS

1. All women need to prepare for some job or profession, even though they may not plan to work outside the home after marriage.
2. Weigh all considerations carefully before selecting the line of training and career you pursue.
3. Work resolutely and professionally toward finding the job you want.

THOUGHTS FOR YOU

1. QUESTIONS
   A. Fill out the sample application form given in the lesson.

   B. If you have ever held a job, tell how you went about securing it.

   C. Discuss some special problems that might confront a Christian working with non-Christians.

   D. What special responsibilities should a Christian feel toward her employer?

2. SCRIPTURES
   Working women.
   Acts 9:36
   Acts 16:14
   Acts 18:2-3
   Proverbs 31:10-31

   Working in God's kingdom.
   1 Thessalonians 4:11
   1 Timothy 2:10
   Titus 2:7
   Titus 3:1
   Ecclesiastes 9:10

   Responsibilities of employees.
   Ephesians 4:28
   Ephesians 6:5-9
   Colossians 3:22-24
   2 Thessalonians 3:10-11
   Titus 3:1
   Ecclesiastes 9:10

Lesson 7

Concerning the Church

DISCOVERY

Your decision-making was at its zenith when you made your choice for Christ. Becoming a member of His body, being saved through obedience to Him—these were peak moments of your life. No doubt you heard many appealing sermons and spent much time in soul-searching before you made your final decision and accepted Jesus as your Savior.

Often, however, great emphasis is placed on initial obedience—repentance, confession, and baptism—while little thought is given to the tremendous opportunities and obligations facing you after you have become a member of the Lord's body, His church. Although rendering obedience to God by becoming a Christian is undeniably important, learning to effectively live the Christian life is likewise important.

Perhaps, like many young Christians, you feel a deep need for greater involvement and commitment to Christ. Unlike some older Christians, you have not yet been assigned a special work by the elders, have not yet found your niche in the work of the church, have not yet discovered how your particular talents might best be used for the Lord. In fact, perhaps you have talents even *you* don't know about yet.

Below are some feelings often shared by young people as Christians. Check those which represent your feelings, then read on to see if this chapter offers any helps to you and your church work.

___I feel that the elders neglect to work enough young people into the church programs.

___I feel that the women are an underused resource of the Lord's church.

___I feel that I should be doing more for God.

___I want to work in a special way in the church's programs—but don't know how to begin.

___I wish to unite our young people on church projects, but get little response.

___I want to be taken more seriously as a productive Christian.

WHAT TO DO?
Becoming a Productive Christian

First of all, you must realize that being a Christian is a personal relationship between you and your God. When you obeyed Him, you promised your life to Him, regardless of what anyone else did or said.

The same is true now. Whether in a large or small, strong or weak congregation, you yourself still have a personal obligation to do all the work you can for Christ and His church. So, in beginning your search for your place in the church, begin in private. Find something for yourself to do. Look for good works others are passing by.

So many Christian works are those done without elders' or sponsors' supervision—those done, in fact, without anyone's knowing it but you, God, and those you help. Where to begin? What can you do privately to work for God? Following are some suggestions. Check those you feel you would like to do sometime soon:

___Visit someone who is sick. Take with you a flower—or better yet, some cupcakes you made yourself.

___Do a good deed for the sick. If the wife and mother is ill, there is ironing, washing, babysitting, dusting to do. Take on a major project: prepare them a full meal, then take it to them hot and fresh.

___Visit someone elderly you know. Sit and talk with him for thirty minutes. Nothing could make an old person happier.

___Go by your local nursing home or home for the aged. Visit several rooms to chat a while.

___Begin at home. Do something unexpectedly nice for your parents.

___Send cards to the sick and aged. These are cheery reminders that only take a moment of your time.

___Spend time reading God's Word to become a more effective Christian.

___Invite your friends and neighbors to go to church services with you.

___Visit your new neighbors; carry them a cake you baked; invite them to worship services.

Supervised Work Under the Elders

Most of the work of the local congregation as a whole is done under the guidance of the elders. Since they are the leaders, they decide where funds go, which projects and programs are currently feasible for the congregation at which they work.

Perhaps you feel your services are being by-passed and your talents overlooked by the elders. What can you do about it? How can you become involved in the supervised program of your congregation? Read on:

___Keep in mind that the elders are over-worked and probably unaware that they are not using you (or young people in general) in the congregation's program.

___Realize that women have a great many roles in church work. Don't feel discriminated against.

___Keep in mind that, if the congregation is sizable, the elders may not know you or may not realize that you wish to get more involved.

___Volunteer your services. Let several elders know that you are willing to work at a special task—or at any task, if you really feel that way.

___Show up at places where you will become known as one willing to work. Go to teacher training classes, zone meetings, church outings and visitation groups.

___Volunteer for jobs others are reluctant to do. Teach in Vacation Bible School; help publish, fold, and mail out the church bulletin; stay after the church picnics to help clean up.

___Do a good job of whatever you do. Soon the elders will have you on so many duties your head will spin.

Young People in Action

Although you are enthusiastic about church work and want your friends to join you in your efforts, they often will not co-operate. The teen-age years are busy ones—dating, school, jobs, all are time consuming. Often young people feel that they have no time for church work. Teen-agers are also sometimes shy—they feel timid about the meetings and contacts with people they will have if they participate in church work.

However, most young people can be persuaded to become more involved. They will need persuasion from a zealous, committed worker—*you*. If you are determined that your Bible School friends should band together as Christians to do church work, here are some things you can do about it.

(1) Let your friends know that church work can be fun. Any time a group of friends meet, they can find fun and good times to share. Remind them how lonely one worker would be folding, stamping, and addressing church bulletins. But an assembly line of friends, gathering to do the same job? More fun; much faster.

(2) Tell your friends that church work is rewarding. The gratitude of the sick and aged; the smiles and delight of orphans; the pride of your parents; most of all, the blessings of God—all of these are the rewards of even the simplest kind deeds.

(3) Enlist the aid of your Sunday School sponsors or the church youth worker. You will need an understanding adult to help you plan your projects, help set up schedules, and give advice. This adult will also be helpful in enlisting volunteers to participate.

Suppose now you have persuaded your friends. Everyone is excited; your class wants to do some good works. Now what can you do, and what planning is involved? Below are some good suggestions for activities and some of the plans you must arrange beforehand. (Be sure to enlist the aid of the teen-age boys. They will be needed and of course welcomed on many of the projects listed below.)

1. *Activity*: Make it your job to take the Lord's Supper to the sick and shut-ins. *Plans*: (1) Ask the deacon in charge of the Communion to provide you with the trays you will take. (2) Practice in advance the songs you will sing, if any. (3) Determine a regular order to the short worship you will conduct. (4) Call ahead to everyone you will visit (except hospital patients) to let them know you are coming.

2. *Activity*: Visit a local nursing home monthly to entertain and chat with the patients. *Plans*: (1) Call ahead to make an appointment, scheduling both a date and a time. (2) Practice songs you will sing. Include some spiritual songs and some older folk songs the patients will remember and enjoy. (3) Carry out a short program, then visit a moment with patients who aren't too sick to appreciate your coming.

3. *Activity*: Visit a local orphan home to play with the children. *Plans*: (1) Call ahead. Arrange a date and time so your visit will not interfere with the schedule of the home. (2) Go casually; be prepared to play whatever games the children would like to play. Have a few ideas of your own, however, if the children can think of nothing to do. (3) While there, set up another time with the supervisor when you can return. (4) If permissible with houseparents and compatible with meal time, take along small favors (bubblegum, suckers) for the children. Be sure to take enough.

4. *Activity*: Plan to help an orphan or orphans. Upon request, most orphans' homes will let a class sponsor a child for a year. (1) Through your classroom contributions, you would supply the child's clothing for twelve months. (2) Or, plan a clothing drive for an entire group of orphans. Through contributions, buy clothing; or you might like to make some of them. (3) A holiday season project is always good. Each member of the class would buy a gift for an orphan. *Plans*: (1) Check with the supervisor; he can tell you how these matters are handled. (2) If a clothing drive is planned, get a list of sex, ages, and sizes from

the supervisor. Attach to each piece of clothing the age, sex, and size for which it was intended. (3) Since your class will be buying for a limited group, be sure the supervisor provides a list of names, ages, sizes, and sex of each child he wishes you to buy for. Check with him about several things: how much money should be spent on each gift (all children should receive gifts of the same value), whether gifts should be wrapped, whether toys or clothing are preferred as gifts. Be sure to follow his instructions. (4) If you provide gifts for specific children, make certain their names are on the gifts intended for them.

5. *Activity*: Cook and deliver meals to all the sick of the congregation. (This is for home patients only.) *Plans*: (1) Call the families to notify them of what you are doing, and when. (2) Have a meeting to arrange the menu. Everyone is assigned a specific food to provide in a certain quantity. (3) If you have a kitchen in your church building, you may meet and cook the meal there, or each person can cook a portion at home. (4) At a designated place, perhaps the church fellowship hall, all food should be brought in non-returnable containers. Food should already be divided into portions for each family. (5) Divide into groups—each group will deliver dinner to one family. (This project may be spread over several days. An attempt to cook too much at once can be disastrous, even for the most experienced cook.)

Be sure not to lose sight of the fact that you are doing all of these things for the glory of God.

A MODERN PARABLE

"Church just doesn't interest me," complained Joe to Patty as they left the Sunday worship service. "I mean, it's so irrelevant."

Patty squinted in the bright sunlight. "What's irrelevant about helping people?"

"Helping people? Ha! You know all we do is congregate, sing a few songs—if you can call *that* singing—and listen to an empty sermon."

Bill had now joined the couple. "Speak for yourself, Joe. Maybe that's all *you* do, but I've been doing some personal work, some visiting..."

"Yeah!" Joe kicked a pebble with his foot and shoved his hands into his pockets. "But I mean the church as a whole! What are we really doing? Tell me that!"

"Well, I baked some cookies for old Mrs. Talmon," contributed Patty, "and Mom and I stop by the nursing home every week."

"My mom is always ironing for someone who's sick," put in Bill. "She's doing something."

"But you're telling me about *individuals!*" cried Joe, exasperated. "What about the church as a whole—what is *it* doing?"

"The church as a whole *is* individuals," Patty said quietly, "and we've told you what we are doing. Now you tell us what *you* are doing."

Joe had no reply.

MORAL: If you think the church should do more, go ahead and do more.

CLOSING THOUGHTS

1. There is congregational responsibility, and there is individual responsibility. Make sure you live a Christian life every day, doing every good work you can find to do.
2. As the elders try to develop congregational responsibility, there is a place for you to work. Offer your services to the elders and work well under their supervision.
3. Be the instigator of some actions and projects in which the young people exclusively will participate. There will be both fun and rewards involved in these activities.

THOUGHTS FOR YOU

1. QUESTIONS
   A. Which do you feel is most important, elder-instigated programs or personal projects you find for yourself? Is either more important?

   B. Which do you do best—individual Christian works or group works?

   C. Of all the Christian works (visiting, teaching, benevolence), which do you feel you can do best for the glory of God? Do you feel that God expects you to work in all aspects of his kingdom? Discuss the parable of the talents (Matthew 25) in connection with this.

2. SCRIPTURES
   Youth in the church.
   Ecclesiastes 12:1
   1 Timothy 4:12

   Working for God.
   Matthew 6:33
   Matthew 25:14-30
   Romans 12:4-15
   Galatians 6:10
   Ephesians 4:11-16

3. With your teacher arrange a class project involving your entire class, along with other youth classes in your congregation, if desired.

4. Choose for yourself several personal projects of good works you would like to begin. Work these into your weekly schedule and try to continue with these good works as long as the opportunity is there.

Lesson 8

Dating: Attraction and Distraction

DISCOVERY

Attracting dates—getting boys to notice you and ask you for a date: this is a problem of the majority of girls everywhere. Somehow, girls begin to notice boys and want to date at a younger age than fellows do. From the beginning of the teen-age years, girls begin to be aware of their personality and physical appearance because they want boys to like them.

The dilemma is this: girls like boys, are attracted to them, want to date them; but society dictates that the boys usually must do the asking. And the fellows don't seem to want to co-operate!

Since it is common knowledge that girls are attracted to the opposite sex and would like to know how to get a proper response from the males, this chapter will deal precisely with that problem. If you can't ask a boy for a date, how do you get him to ask you for one? How do you get boys to notice you, to like you? How much prompting and encouraging should the girl do in order to get a date? These and other questions will be dealt with.

First of all, look over the chart below. Check the sentiments or problems that are yours, then read further into the chapter for some ideas to help you.

___I am a fairly attractive girl, but boys don't notice me.
___I am not very attractive, but have lots of good qualities. If only boys would give me a chance, I think they'd like me.
___I don't know where to meet some boys to date. None of the fellows I know appeal to me.
___I would like to meet some boys on blind dates but wonder if this is wise.

WHAT TO DO?
Attracting Boys

First of all, a few preliminary points need to be made in connection with this subject: (1) Attracting boys is not a goal in itself. The object is for a Christian girl to find Christian dates in a Christian way. And, of course, the object of dating is to find a future marriage partner.

(2) Although physical appearance should be strongly stressed (everyone should look as good as she can), the Christian girl should continue to stress even more strongly those personality and character traits which make her a true Christian. (3) If physical appearance is not one of your stronger qualities, you should realize two things: you will probably work even harder to be a likable person because of this; mature men (not always boys) realize the worth of the person despite either attractive or not-quite-so-attractive looks.

Keeping these things in mind, read the following general suggestions about how to attract the right kind of dates. More specific ideas will follow.

1. *Look your best.* Possibly this sounds like old advice or just common sense to you. But you'd be surprised how many girls go out for just a few minutes looking their absolute worst and, as fate would have it, have chanced upon a very attractive male. (How were you to know that a new check-out boy was working at that little supermarket? And you just in from washing the car!) So looking your best is a matter of special care not only on dates but on any quick trip you make anywhere.

Too, looking your best involves experiments with make-up and hair styles. While it is possible to be too engrossed in your own looks, many girls somewhat neglect their appearance. Many average-looking girls could look definitely *nice,* and many nice-looking girls could become *pretty* by adopting a more complimentary hair style or spending more time with make-up.

2. *Be yourself,* but be your best self. (Remember that personality makeover you did in chapter one?) Although everyone has a best side to show others, you should strive to become a genuine, likable person at all times. Relax, smile, be friendly. Pretending and putting on an act for others (either boys or girls) is easily detected by those who observe you. Characterize yourself by being the same person to everyone, everywhere. If you have properly developed your personality, you should not have to change it for the purpose of getting dates.

3. *Do not be silly.* Although boys appreciate a girl with a good sense of humor, they despise girlish, foolish actions. Above all, do not stoop to the adolescent game of giggling. Fellows think (and are correct in their belief) that silly, girlish behavior is a sign of immaturity and lack of womanliness.

4. *Do not pull stunts to get attention.* In the course of attracting boys, you will naturally want them to focus their attention on you. However, pulling stunts is a poor way to get attention; the attention you receive will not be the kind that you want.

Now that a few appearance and behavior guides have been given, the more specific question comes again: "Well, how *do* you get boys to notice you and ask you for a date?" Below are some positive ways you can attract the boy you wish to date:

1. *Do be a lady and a Christian.* Make no mistake about it: boys prefer Christian girls. Think of it: even the roughest fellows you know like to date nice girls. (True, they may date not-so-nice girls for a short while—but not for long.)

The type of boy you are trying to attract should be a Christian; therefore, you as a Christian lady will appeal to him. If you do not, then certainly the boy and not your Christian ideals should be sacrificed.

2. *Do go where the boys are.* There are many places where the boys are to be found, and these places vary from town to town. In your town, perhaps the fellows congregate on Saturday night at the skating rink, or the bowling alley—even the local pizza place. Although it is inadvisable to go to a place where *only* boys are to be found, the above-mentioned places are public accommodations for both male and female.

So—take a girlfriend along with you (*one* friend, not a flock. A flock scares the boys away.) Go bowling, or skating, or whatever. Have a good time and be yourself. You'll be noticed. But get in there and skate or bowl—don't stand on the sidelines like a tigress stalking the prey. Soon you'll meet some of the boys there. Then the rest is up to them.

3. *Do let the boys take the initiative.* Like it or not, there are certain standards in our American society which dictate that, in most cases, the boys ask the girl for a date. Although you may not like this rule, it is generally best to abide by it.

Therefore, however much you may be around a boy, no matter how many little tactics you may use to get him to notice you—it is considered *his* place to ask you out.

4. *Do be friendly.* This is a good Christian principle, and there is nothing wrong with applying it to boys as well as girls. Smile and speak to fellows you meet. Let them realize that you're a nice person to know, and they'll want to know you!

5. *Do have a sense of humor.* Boys are drawn to girls who can joke, laugh, and have a good time. Being too serious too soon can scare off a boy. Learn to have fun with different people, see the funny and bright side of life. The sound of your genuine laughter may attract a boy.

6. *Do be sensible about blind dates.* What does that mean? Read below some rules for blind dates in a nutshell.

(1) Soliciting a blind date can be one of the best and easiest ways to meet a boy.

(2) Be sure to talk it over with your mother. Let her know that you intend to abide by the following rules (rules 3-6).

(3) Ask a Christian dating couple to get you a date with a boy that they know to be nice. It is generally better for the boy to ask the other boy, rather than for the girl to ask him.

(4) At least on the first date (maybe the second, too) double date with the couple who got you the date with the boy.

(5) If he turns out not to be the nice boy the other couple thought he was, do not go with him again.

(6) Do not go on a blind date alone with the boy. If the situation arises where the other couple cannot go along, then stay home, pop some popcorn, and watch a movie on the VCR.

7. *Do handle calmly and carefully any approach a boy makes.* Suppose at a skating rink a boy introduces himself to you, you talk a while, and he asks to take you home. What do you do?

(1) Say "no." You do not know him, your parents have never met him, and you would be taking a risk. But there are different ways of saying "no."

(2) If you do not ever want to date this boy, just say, "No, thanks." Be sure not to give him your address or telephone number, since he may call and waste your time and his.

(3) If you would like to date him sometime, say, "Sorry, I came with Stephanie. Some other time, though, would be nice." That gives him an opener to ask for your telephone number so he can call you for a date.

(4) If the boy is definitely not the nice type, and he's making suggestions, being a complete pest, then squelch him with your most icy tone of voice. You don't need a character like that hanging around.

A MODERN PARABLE

Karla and Renee were bowling well that Saturday night—in fact, having so much fun that they didn't notice that two handsome fellows had taken the lane next to them.

Finally Karla glanced up and caught one of the boys looking at her. Quickly he looked away, but she saw him say something to the other boy who gave her a stealthy glance.

Then it was her turn to bowl. Luckily the ball rolled dead center for a beautiful strike. "Great!" called Renee.

"Sure was," they heard a male voice say. Turning, Karla found one of the boys from the next lane grinning at her. "You must bowl pretty often."

"Occasionally," she smiled, "but that strike was only luck."

"Oh?" He raised his eyebrows. "My pal, Brandon, used to bowl in a league. He says you bowl like a pro."

"In a league?" cried Renee. "Maybe you could give us a few pointers, then."

"Sure." Both boys crossed over to the girls' lane. "By the way, I'm Rick Drake, and this is Brandon Miller. Who are you?"

MORAL: Take up bowling.

CLOSING THOUGHTS

1. Although a girl usually does not ask a boy for a date, she can do her best to get boys to notice and like her.
2. Looking, and being, the best person you can will attract boys.
3. Incorporating Christian attitudes into your life will make you more attractive.
4. Be sure you date only the nicest boys you can find.

THOUGHTS FOR YOU

1. QUESTIONS
   A. If you have ever set out to attract a boy who had never noticed you, tell how you went about it. Were the results successful? If not, tell what you think you did wrong.

   B. What quality more than any other do you feel attracts boys to girls?

   C. If boys have not been noticing you, can you from this chapter discover what might be a reason for their neglect? What quality or attitude do you most need to improve?

2. SCRIPTURES
   1 Samuel 16:7
   Proverbs 17:22
   Ecclesiastes 3:11
   Matthew 23:27
   1 Peter 3:3-4

Lesson 9

Dating: From the First Date to the Last

DISCOVERY

Your first date with any boy is an exciting event. A girl never knows when any new date she is having might be *the* date that will lead to serious courtship and eventually, marriage.

Not only is preparation important (looking your most attractive self), but your actions become a concern: How do I act? What will I say? What will he say? How will he act? Anxieties—quite natural ones, really, begin to plague a girl. Little things like—should I sit next to the door? what if my arm misses the sleeve when he helps me on with my coat? what will I do with my chewing gum at the restaurant? what if there's a deadly silence and neither of us can think of anything to say?—these problems confront a girl on the first date.

The first date may progress to many more, however. Liking may develop into loving, and more serious questions about love, necking, petting, may enter a girl's mind. This chapter is intended to guide the girl from her first date through the last—so every girl, the one who hasn't dated or the one who is engaged, may find it helpful.

WHAT TO DO?
Dating

Getting ready for an evening with someone you've never dated before is quite an experience. What to do and how to act: these two questions are your main concerns on that first date. Look over the guidelines below, designed to help you through a first date with any boy:

1. *Look good; dress appropriately.* When in doubt about where you're going, a nice pair of slacks and blouse should take you almost anywhere.

2. *Do not worry beforehand about what to say;* this will make things worse because it will make you nervous. Besides, if you think up a list of things to say, you may talk too much, and most boys detest chattering.

3. *Talk about what interests the boy,* but don't be false about it. If he's a football fan and you don't know a thing about it, don't pretend that you do. Your ignorance on the subject will quickly be evident.

(Besides, this will give him an opportunity to teach you all about football—and *that* supplies more conversation.)

4. *Don't do anything because you feel the boy expects it.* Instead of worrying about "What will he think of me if I don't sit close to him, kiss him goodnight, etc.," let *him* worry about what *you* will think if he does so-and-so. You can put him in this position by being a lady and putting yourself as a trusted responsibility to him. Care enough about yourself to respect yourself and he will respect you. Then he will ask himself, "What does *she* expect of *me*?" rather than vice versa.

5. *Don't die of heart failure if you make a mistake.* Every first date contains its share of tragedies: the spilt milkshake, the stumble outside on the steps, the backward sentence. Just use your sense of humor and laugh it off. One mistake won't condemn you—or him.

6. *Don't ask, "Will I see you again?"* That's his line, remember?

Above are listed general hints about a first date. However, maybe other dates have followed the first. And one ever-present question that girls think about (although they may not ask it aloud) is, "What about kissing?" Since this is an important question, several comments are given below which are intended to help you put kissing in perspective.

1. *Keep in mind that no relationship hinges entirely upon a kiss.* Girls would worry a lot less and enjoy themselves more if they wouldn't constantly feel that a kiss at a certain time is necessary or expected.

2. *Make up your mind what a kiss means to you;* no one else can make up your mind for you. Then regulate your actions according to what you decide.

3. *Do not attach too much importance to the other party's kiss.* Even if you have decided that a kiss is meaningful to you, do not assume that every boy who wants to kiss you is ready for a meaningful relationship. A kiss may not mean to him what it does to you.

4. If you decide that you are going to kiss a boy, *decide how much you are going to kiss him.* If you don't make this decision, he will.

5. *Some connotations of a kiss:* A kiss is for pleasure. Too much kissing can lead to too much pleasure. A kiss is the touching of lips, nothing else. A kiss from you will mean a lot to someone special someday, and he probably will be jealous of anyone else you may've kissed.

6. *Make the time and the place right.* There is a world of difference between a goodnight kiss on your front porch and a clench in a parked car.

7. *If a girl is interesting in ways other than just physically,* boys will not feel it necessary to neck constantly. If you can't hold his interest any other way, your personality needs a major overhaul.

Perhaps the above comments were too basic for you. Maybe you are in love and thinking of marriage. If so, you may be confronted with a more perplexing problem than "to kiss or not to kiss."

A common problem of all couples in love is that of refraining from petting and sexual intimacy. Although you feel a physical need and attraction for your fiance (which is a natural impulse of love), you know that marriage is the only proper place for a sexual relationship.

If you have been wondering about petting, then wonder no more. Not only is this unspiritual (see scriptures in *Thoughts for You* section), it is a dangerous practice for your mental well-being. Many girls feel that pregnancy is the only unwelcome result of petting and pre-marital intercourse. Not so. In fact, petting without intercourse has its special dangers: If you and your boyfriend pet without indulging in the act of lovemaking (the natural post-requisite to petting), you are thwarting and frustrating your natural emotions. This can lead to anxiety, depression, guilt feelings, mal-adjustment or even partial impotency in marriage. The body, frustrated too often by petting sessions without the natural follow-up, may refuse to carry out satisfactorily the sexual act in marriage.

Therefore, look not only at the unspirituality of petting, but at the bad physical and mental reactions that may result. You will feel and be a much better person if you go to the marriage altar pure beside your mate.

"But I'm in love!" you may cry. "My fiance and I really want to wait until we're married to indulge in intimacy, but how do we refrain?" Some suggestions:

1. Keep in mind the person you want to be. Read the Bible and pray that God will help you remain pure.

2. Stay in crowds. Double-date, go to parties, be with friends as much as possible. That way, intimate contact is impossible.

3. *Never* sit in a parked car. Without a seed a plant cannot grow. Likewise, without a beginning, petting cannot develop.

4. Don't schedule idle hours. Plan something to do with your evening, then do it.

If a girl begins her dating in the right way, she will most likely remain the right kind of person.

Develop a self-image. Decide who you are, what you are like, and what your actions will be. Then act accordingly, careful not to let anyone tear down the self-hood you have constructed. People will respect you for your standards even though they may not agree with them.

Continue to keep yourself pure throughout your engagement. A betrothal is special and meaningful and can be such a holy and happy time if you do not besmear you character by hasty actions. By guarding your emotions and preserving your purity until marriage, you are guaranteeing a happier life for yourself and your fiance. So from the first date to the last, be yourself, be pure, be God's.

A MODERN PARABLE

Teresa was troubled. Tossing to and fro in bed, unable to sleep, she thought about her date with Drew that night. They were engaged to be married next month, and both were so excited about finally being together in a home of their own.

However, every date turned out to be a struggle of conscience. No matter how hard they tried, it seemed so natural to be in one another's arms that they found it increasingly hard to refrain from sexual intimacy.

Tonight they had come home early from their date, deciding that maybe Drew should leave earlier. "What can I do?" thought Teresa. "We want this last month to be so happy."

Suddenly an image rose before her: a close friend of hers who was already married. This lady was a wonderful Christian in every way. "Why, I can't imagine her in a parked car, necking or petting," thought Teresa, "and that's just the kind of person I want to be."

She turned over, feeling some relief. "Drew and I can wait," she told herself, "because we know the kind of people we want to be. And the kind of people we want to be remain pure and wholesome throughout life." Smiling, Teresa closed her eyes, knowing that her married friend could never know what a wonderful inspiration she had been.

MORAL: Be ye followers of others, as they are of Christ.

CLOSING THOUGHTS

1. A first date is usually exciting and anxiety ridden, but take all the steps you can to make it a fun experience.
2. As dating progresses, keep your standards before you and act accordingly. Do not let worries over-shadow the fun of dating.
3. Especially in the engagement period, the problem of a deeper physical relationship may arise. Keep in mind your Christian ideals to guide your actions.

THOUGHTS FOR YOU

1. QUESTIONS
   A. Recount the experience of your first date. Tell of some tragic or humorous happenings.

   B. Tell why dating for a physical relationship alone might hamper you truly getting to know your dates.

   C. There are many reasons why petting is unwise. Cite some reasons that you personally feel as to why it is not a good practice.

2. SCRIPTURES
   Admonitions; proper use of body
   Proverbs 31:10
   Matthew 5:8
   1 Corinthians 6:19-20
   1 Thessalonians 4:7
   1 Timothy 5:22

Lesson 10

Marriage: Choosing a Mate

DISCOVERY

The process of choosing the person you will marry is a challenging one. While some may lead you to believe that deciding whom to marry is an easy task, this is not always the case. True, love is a very important requirement of a happy and successful marriage. This is not the only requirement, however, as evidenced by the thousands of divorces obtained by people who were "in love" when they married.

This chapter is one which contains advice often unheeded. It will view in perspective the various qualities and emotions which enter into the choosing of a life-long mate. If you will study it diligently, surely your dating days will be more carefree and happy.

Most girls date with the idea that someday they will marry. Therefore, the task of the girl is to eliminate undesirable males from her life until she finds the one with whom she is ready to share the entirety of her life. This is a serious, awesome step—but there are ways to practically ensure that your choice for a husband will not be the wrong one. With your well-being and happiness in mind, this chapter is written.

WHAT TO DO?
Choosing a Mate

As you develop as a Christian woman, there are many attitudes forming in your mind. One of these attitudes is your attitude toward marriage. A major step in the right direction is for you to form proper and godly attitudes toward marriage. Read carefully the thoughts below. These feelings should have found a place in your heart. Check those you would like to think about some more.

___Marriage is instituted of God, thus is holy. In the very beginning, God gave Eve to Adam and instructed them that they were then "one flesh." A holy relationship signifies that two holy people be partners in that relationship. Because marriage is holy, it cannot be regarded lightly.

___Marriage is forever. God instructed that man should not put asunder what He had joined together. In fact, it is impossible to

63

do so. When you think of marriage, never consider it as a trial and error experiment. The old adage "try, try again" has no bearing upon re-marriage. Your responsibility is to choose your mate wisely, carefully, and prayerfully, determined that your first marriage will be your last.

___Marriage is based on lasting emotions. While fleeting love is enjoyable, it is not a solid foundation for a marriage. Make sure that a lasting, growing love for your husband-to-be precedes any marriage vows. Mutual honor, respect, and consideration must also be present in a happy marriage.

___Marriage is not a panacea for all of your problems. Some girls feel that all responsibilities, rules, and regulations end with marriage. If parents are strict, they may think of marriage as an escape. But marriage is not an escape—marriage binds you. While the ties of marriage are a joy to those who realize what married life involves, they could be a hateful restriction to a girl who enters a marriage merely to escape.

If you can understand all of the above, then perhaps you are ready to begin your choice of a lifelong mate. Below are listed some ways in which you can improve your chances of selecting for yourself a husband with whom you can be happy and fulfilled.

1. *Date only Christian boys.* By doing this, you are guaranteeing that you will marry a Christian. True, the number of dates you have may decrease, since Christian boys are sometimes difficult to find. But which is more important—having huge numbers of dates or ensuring that you will not fall in love with a non-Christian?

Keep in mind that, though extremely important, marriage is only one transient facet of this life. The ultimately important thing is that you get to heaven. Therefore, it would be foolish to risk falling in love with someone who—after marriage—might hinder or jeopardize your living the Christian life.

If you marry a Christian, you should be able to obey the Biblical command given to wives: "be in subjection to your own husbands," without fear that he would ask you to do anything wrong. Too, the indifference of a non-Christian husband has caused many Christian wives to fall away from God.

Seen in the light of eternity, dating and marrying a Christian is so very important, since both of you may help one another to live better lives.

2. *Be sure you are in love.* Often girls wonder how to tell if the love they feel for a boy is the true and lasting kind. One of the best ways is to give your love the test of time.

There is no way to tell true love in a short time. A few weeks does not give you time to get to know a boy well enough to know if you can love him forever. Date him at least six months before you become engaged; then date him six months before you're married. Then, if you still both love each other after knowing what you do about each other, go ahead and marry.

3. *Be sure your feelings for your mate-to-be include more than love.* While love is wonderful, an entire marriage cannot exist upon love alone. Do the two of you have mutual trust, respect, and honor for one another? Do you like each other, as well as love each other? If none of these feelings is present, your marriage foundation will be shaky.

4. *You and your fiance should share interests.* Although no two people like exactly the same things, it is imperative that you and your husband have mutual interests so that your leisure time can be spent together. Far too many husbands go fishing or golfing every week-end with the fellows—while the wife sits home alone. If no hobbies or interests are shared, you may become a "week-end widow," totally left out of many of your husband's activities.

5. *The two of you should agree on major matters concerning your marriage.* How do both of you feel about children? If you plan to have a family, how soon? How many? What about the household budget? Will you work after marriage? Will you two have a joint checking account, or will you, the wife, have to make it on an allowance? What about recreational spending? Will one of you balk at going out to eat or to a movie occasionally? What about in-laws?

So many questions that never trouble a dating couple will be yours and your fiance's when you become engaged. Make sure the above questions are settled between the two of you *before* you marry.

6. *Your personality should be compatible with your husband's.* Although there are exceptions, most people are happiest around other people who are like themselves. A stay-at-home husband and a party-hopping wife simply may not find a compatible life together. A joking, continually laughing husband might not find a more serious girl to be a suitable wife. Consider not only the infatuation and excitement of dating; think of the many years ahead you will be spending with this person.

7. *Choose a dependable mate.* Needless to say, you and your husband will encounter many obstacles and problems in your life together. Therefore, you need a husband with a level head, good judgment, and steady character. You need a mate who will hold down a job—not one who is constantly changing jobs and locations, often not working at all. When tragedy strikes, you need a dependable man

to be a steadying force in your life—not a man unable to cope with life's realities.

8. *Make sure you both are ready for marriage.* Marriage means giving up certain things, and taking on the responsibility of other things. If you or your boyfriend feel that you need to be fancy-free a bit longer, don't get married yet. If marriage seems to be a noose rather than a tie of love, put off marriage for a while. Marriage is a life-time proposition and each party must be mature and ready. Marriage is not for the immature or unprepared. Make sure you are through with other boys; your fiance should be through with other girls.

Your fiance should have a steady job; a place to live should be available (a place for just the two of you); money for daily needs must be accessible. Don't enter marriage until both of you are ready and prepared.

As you are dating, considering different boys as possible choices for marriage, try to use sound judgment. Follow both the head and the heart: follow neither to the exclusion of the other.

A MODERN PARABLE

"Hi, Elaine!" Leanne stopped on the sidewalk to greet her old school friend. "I haven't seen you in ages." Looking closely at Elaine, she saw that age had registered on her friend's face since she had last seen her.

"Leanne! I was thinking about you just the other day! Heard you've got a beautiful diamond."

Shyly yet proudly, Leanne held out her hand. "Yes. Jim gave it to me two weeks ago. We'll get married this spring."

"It's beautiful," Elaine said, with something like a sigh. "It's been three years since Lance and I were married—I can hardly remember what it was like to be young and in love."

"Why, Elaine! You know you love Lance!"

"Yes, I do." She looked away. "But we were so young—I was still in high school. And we're still living with his parents until he can finish college...Well—tell me, where will you and Jim live?"

"Oh, we've been looking at houses for days. Jim's been saving his money for years—just waiting for a girl like me to come along, he says."

"Waiting..." A sad smile crossed Elaine's face. "Yes, maybe waiting is the best thing. Here you've had a few years of freedom, worked and bought some nice clothes. Jim's already finished college and has been working and saving."

Her friend's sad face dimmed some of Leanne's excitement. "I'm sorry, Elaine, if things aren't working out as well as you'd like..."

"Oh, don't worry about me." She straightened her shoulders. "But some of us do get in a hurry, don't we?"

MORAL: Surely you can guess the moral of this one!

CLOSING THOUGHTS

1. Before you think of choosing a mate or getting married, you should realize what marriage is and what it is not.
2. Follow wisdom and good judgment in choosing the one with whom you will spend the remainder of your life.
3. Be sure you both are ready for marriage before you take your final vows.

THOUGHTS FOR YOU

1. QUESTIONS
   A. At what age do you feel most girls are mature enough to marry? Cite reasons.

   B. Suppose military service or a college education delays your fiance's plans to get a job and provide an income. Should an adjustment of marriage plans be made?

   What alternatives are there to postponing the wedding?

   C. What disadvantages might there be to marrying just prior to a long period of separation (such as military service)? Are there any advantages?

   D. What special traits are you looking for in a husband?

2. SCRIPTURES
   Holiness of marriage.
   Genesis 2:24
   Hebrews 13:4

   Endurance of marriage.
   Genesis 2:24
   Matthew 19:3-9
   1 Corinthians 7:39

   Responsibilities of marriage.
   Ephesians 5:22,24,33
   1 Corinthians 7:5
   Titus 2:4-5

   Compatibility required.
   Amos 3:3
   2 Corinthians 6:14-18

Lesson 11

Marriage: Preparing to Wed

DISCOVERY

Once a couple become engaged to marry, there are seemingly endless details to which they must attend. Besides the wedding ceremony, minister, bridesmaids, reception, and invitations, you must prepare yourself in many ways to become a bride.

Personal preparation is extremely important: there is a great transition to be made between the life you have lived as a single girl and the life you will experience as a married woman. Many brides would find the change less traumatic if they would attend to personal preparation before they are married.

Too, preparation of the wedding is important. If planned carefully and over a period of time, the planning stage of your wedding can be exciting and enjoyable. Give yourself time to enjoy your preparation. Don't rush or hurry things. Since you'll be married for the rest of your life, there's no great hurry under usual circumstances (barring military service and similar things).

This chapter will deal in two segments with the preparations needed before the wedding. Whether large or small, may your wedding be memorable and only a foretaste of the marital bliss that can be yours and your mate's.

WHAT TO DO?
Preparing for the Ceremony

Several months before your wedding, you should begin to plan for it. Although you may have only a small ceremony, there are still many details to be taken care of.

First of all, you should (with your family and fiance) determine the size of your wedding party. With this in mind, you will then select the place where you wish to be married. If this is a church building, you should check with the minister, secretary, or caretaker of that church. Probably you will need to reserve the building for two nights (that of your rehearsal and your wedding), so be sure to do this well in advance and *before* you print invitations! There may be a small charge for the use of the facilities at the church building.

After this preliminary is decided, you are free to plan your wedding with the certainty that your wedding can be held at that church building on the night you planned. Then you can begin to do the following: (Depending upon the size of your wedding, of course, you may eliminate some of the ideas below.)

1. *Choose your bridesmaids and maid of honor.* With them decide the type and color of dresses they will wear. If you plan to have their dresses made, you should choose the pattern and material in plenty of time so that fittings will not be rushed.

2. *Ask your fiance to select his best man and ushers.* Be sure to tell them what to wear for the wedding. If you decide that they must wear tuxedos, instruct them of a near-by rental service where they can be fitted well in advance.

3. *Solicit the services of a minister.* Since most ministers are very busy, be sure to check early with your minister so that he may put your wedding on his schedule. He should also be told the rehearsal date since he must be present there.

4. *Compile a guest list and order invitations.* Most printers have many samples from which you both may choose your invitation. If you do not feel that the size of your wedding (or budget) merits the use of printed or engraved invitations, you might have a general invitation read to the congregation with which you and your fiance worship.

5. *Order flowers, candles, arrangements.* Although most florists can operate on short notice, it is best to check ahead of time about your wedding arrangements. Decide beforehand exactly what you would like (don't forget the reception) and discuss this with the florist. If some close friend or a relative can manage it, the arrangements will probably cost a good deal less if picked up at the shop. If the florist does the delivering and arranging of the flowers, the cost will be more.

Be sure to order flowers for: yourself, all attendants, corsages for all serving girls at the reception, corsages for the mothers, and boutonnieres for all male members of the wedding party.

6. *Order your wedding cake.* Do not order a cake too large. By calculating the number of people who will be at the reception, you can get the baker to accommodate that number. If you wish a catered reception, you should notify the caterer of exactly what you desire and of the date and time of the reception. By arranging your own reception, however, you will be saving on cost.

Decide on a color scheme, then get flowers, tablecloths, and punch to contribute to this scheme. Check ahead with a china rental service if you will need extra serving plates and punch cups. After you order the cake, be sure to ask the baker when someone can call for it. Don't be caught without your cake!

7. *Shop for your dress.* Your wedding dress will always be a treasure to you. However, keep your budget in mind. Do not spend extravagantly for a wedding gown if you do not have the funds. Choose a gown that pleases you and suits your personality. Also check about a veil—or borrow one from a friend, as many do.

8. *Choose and organize the servers* for your reception. Perhaps you have a close friend who will see to the details of your reception. Arranging the tables, making punch, serving guests—all of this must be done by someone other than you. The servers will serve the cake and punch and collect dishes from guests.

9. If there are friends who wish to give you a *bridal shower or tea,* arrange a date suitable both to you and to them. You should help compile the guest list for the occasion. Don't forget to write a sincere note of thanks to each gift-giver as soon as possible!

10. *Decide on music for the wedding.* Organs, pianos, records, tape recordings—any of these may be used. Unless your congregation owns a musical instrument for such occasions, you must rent an instrument, plus pay the instrumentalist. If your budget is limited, a record or recording would be ideal.

With your fiance, choose the songs you would like to have played before and during the ceremony.

11. *Arrange unusual details.* If you wish your wedding to be different or special in any way, plan this ahead of time. Then explain your wishes to the minister on the night of the rehearsal.

12. *Think of gifts for attendants.* If your wedding is a large one, you may wish to give tokens of appreciation to the bridesmaids and maid of honor.

13. *Marriage license and a blood test* should be obtained in advance. Check with the courthouse at your local county seat to find out the state laws concerning these two items. Many states require the blood test to be taken three days before the marriage license can be obtained; therefore, you must plan ahead!

Whether large or small, your wedding will be something to always remember. Plan it well and enjoy your planning. It is hoped that, no matter what type of wedding you have, some of the above advice will be useful to you.

Personal Preparations for the Wedding

In the busy schedule you will have before your wedding, take time out to do several things:

1. *Have a thorough physical examination.* In this way you can ensure your health and your well-being. If you and your fiance wish

to postpone having children, discuss methods of contraception with your doctor and have him prescribe one.

2. *Overhaul your old wardrobe.* Throw out those ragged underclothes and give little sister (or an orphanage) those clothes you've outgrown. Take this opportunity to begin a neater stage of appearance.

3. *Prepare for your honeymoon.* Pack your suitcase well ahead of time. Plan where you will go. Read a good sex manual, if you feel it will help you or give you confidence.

4. *Make sure you can care for a home.* Here is a list of things you should be able to do well. Check those you can do:

___plan a menu   ___clean windows and floors
___cook a meal   ___wash and iron clothes
___wash dishes   ___make beds

Discuss with your fiance divisions of chores, especially if you both will be working. Keeping house is much easier when the two of you pitch in!

5. *Become better friends with God.* Spend more time in prayer; let Him give you confidence and strength in this time of excitement and anxious moments. Ask Him to help you learn to become a good wife, become a better Christian, and make your husband happy.

With all of these things in mind, approach your wedding. Your excitement will sweep you along; moments of doubt and fright will overtake you. But keep your love for your fiance foremost in mind, and be aware that a greater One is with you. May God bless you in your hour of happiness.

A MODERN PARABLE

Months earlier, Karen had dreamed of this moment. Now it had come. The organ music beckoned her down the aisle to where Ray was standing.

Almost floating, she started down the aisle. Everyone was looking at her. "I," she thought, "I am the bride! Unbelievable!" She caught Ray's eyes and found them full of love for her. "Dear God," she prayed, "help me make him a good wife."

"Karen." Her father's voice echoed in her mind. It had been a month ago when he'd had a fatherly chat with her. "We hope you and Ray will be very happy," he had said. "But a beautiful wedding doesn't guarantee a beautiful marriage. You know that, don't you?"

"I know."

"You and Ray will have to make your own happiness—you'll have to work at it—cause it to happen. Don't let the wedding ceremony be the end of the beauty in your life with Ray."

The voice faded away and the minister's voice was suddenly in her ears. "Dearly beloved, we are gathered here in the presence of God and these witnesses..."

Eyes beaming, she looked at Ray and smiled. "We'll be happy," her heart whispered. "We'll make it happen."

MORAL: It doesn't matter how or where you marry—but whom you marry is important.

CLOSING THOUGHTS

1. Prepare early for the marriage ceremony itself; attend to all details.
2. Make sure you are personally prepared to marry.
3. You should be physically, emotionally, and mentally ready to marry; if you are not, call off the wedding.

THOUGHTS FOR YOU

1. QUESTIONS
   A. What kind of wedding do you plan to have?

   B. List some reasons why the wedding ceremony itself is important and to be cherished.

   C. Why is the time just prior to your wedding a vital and ideal time to draw closer to God?

2. SCRIPTURES
   Consider and keep your vows.
   Proverbs 20:25
   Proverbs 24:27
   Ecclesiastes 5:4

   Read and consider:
   Song of Solomon

Lesson 12

Marriage: The Christian Home

DISCOVERY

When the wedding ceremony is over, the honeymoon has drawn to a close, and the married couple return to their home—this is when the building of a marriage really begins.

In the dating stage of a relationship, couples are prone to overlook the faults, annoying habits, and mannerisms of each other—or perhaps not know about them at all. Not so in a marriage. Living with someone day after day brings to light all the good *and* bad characteristics of that person. Therefore, a good marriage must be built upon acceptance of the other person, not upon an attempt to change him.

Especially in the early months of a marriage, adjustments may be difficult. Unaccustomed to living together, each party may desire to do things his own way. The wife may find her cooking unacceptable to her husband; quarrels may arise over trivia; even the issue of whether or not to leave the daily paper in one piece may cause strife.

So how does a couple rise above the tensions and strains of the early days of marriage? How do they reach a platform of compromise and compatibility? How do they finally reconcile their differences and learn to live together as one? All of this enters into building a Christian home—and this chapter is devoted exclusively to promoting peace and good will in the home.

WHAT TO DO?
How Christians Build a Home

There is hardly anything more frustrating than the discovery of a bride that the man she married is not perfect. In fact, marriage is sometimes so disillusioning that many marriages do not last for even a year. Below are some suggestions to help you avoid the problems that often accompany being newly wed.

1. *Use the first few months of marriage getting to know your husband better.* Do not spend time condemning what he does—make efforts to understand why he does it. Realize that all differences do not mean that one of you is right and the other is wrong; they merely signify that the two of you have different opinions.

2. *Learn your husband's preferences.* Don't insist on performing things the way your mother used to—and he probably won't suggest your doing them the way his mother did. (True! He probably won't!) There may be favorite dishes he prefers a certain way; be sure to cook them. A bit later, slip in a few improvements of your own here and there—he'll notice, all right, and most likely compliment them. If he doesn't, go ahead and cook them his way. A dish of food isn't worth a quarrel.

If you both work, divide up the housekeeping chores. Is he good at lawn work? Does he hate to scrub floors? If you can agree on who will do which duties, keeping your home neat will be much easier.

You'll be surprised how little these decisions will matter to him when he discovers that you're perfectly willing to do it his way. After all, pleasing him is what you want, and what difference do such trivial things make? Not enough to cause anger or strife!

3. *Learn to control your temper.* Logically, there cannot be an argument if one of you refuses to argue. Although disagreements will certainly arise, they can be smoothed out comfortably without one harsh word.

When things do not please you, first determine if the matters are even worth mentioning (perhaps you were being a bit immature). If the issue is worth mentioning, then do just that: mildly, calmly *mention* it. No need for tears or hysterics.

4. *Make friends with your husband's family.* Don't enter the marriage with a defensive attitude toward his family (he's *mine*, not *theirs*). Naturally, he will love and want to be around his family at times, just as you will feel about yours. But assuming that they will try to steal him from you is an immature and unwise attitude.

If your husband wanted to be with his family constantly, he wouldn't have married you. So, first of all, you can be confident and assured of his love. From your vantage point, then, you can approach his family with love. Most mothers love their sons and are very happy to see them marry a Christian girl. If you are so unfortunate as to have a possessive mother-in-law, however, try to be magnanimous. Most likely you won't be seeing much of her. If she should become too great a problem, discuss it with your husband and let him talk with his mother.

5. *Remember your marriage vows.* When you promised to love and obey, for better or for worse, you meant it. So abide by your promise. All marriages have problems, and each new bride has shed tears over her adult responsibilities which she cannot push away. But, the bad times in a good marriage are few. If you love your husband and realize that you are not living in a fairy tale, you will become increasingly adept at handling his moods and all facets of marriage in general.

If problems become too great, consult a minister, your physician, or someone who can help you with that particular problem. Do not let issues continue to build until they become insurmountable.

6. *Do not be a jealous wife.* Nothing in a woman is more unattractive than jealousy. Of course, all women are possessive to some degree and could hardly be expected to control all jealous feelings.

However, being jealous of all women who enter your husband's life will only make you both miserable—and may drive him away from you. Secretaries, clerks, waitresses, old friends, wives of acquaintances—all of these will be around your husband every day. So, control that jealous impulse! Remember, *you* are the one your husband loves, and you are the one he married.

7. *Don't be overly critical.* Ego-destroying criticism is not part of a good marriage. Criticize sparingly and with a deep sense of love, since often even those we love find criticism hard to take. Many times criticism is either given or taken in the wrong spirit; i.e., it is given in a derogatory way or else it is believed by the recipient to express a contempt for him instead of a reproof for his actions.

When you are tempted to correct or criticize, think over what you are about to say—and how you would feel if someone said that to you. Then decide whether or not the criticism is warranted.

8. *Be determined to build a good marriage.* The right attitude will carry you a long way. If you commit your mind and heart to the loving task of making a Christian home, hardly anything can stop you. Work toward your goal with your husband, and your determination will remove any obstacles.

9. *Let God be the third party in your marriage.* Since He has led you to the happiness you now enjoy with a Christian husband, how could you ever forsake Him? Make regular worship and good works an integral part of your life together.

You will find that the Christian attributes you both possess will make your marriage happier. For instance, if you are "slow to anger" as admonished by the Bible, there should be less tension and arguing. If you are "kind...tenderhearted" as instructed by God's Word, see how blissful life can be.

By living as God would have you, your marriage will be more successful and much happier than most.

A MODERN PARABLE

Kelly smiled at Justin as she served him their dinner. "Just think!" she said. "Two whole weeks since we were married." Sitting beside him, she took a bite of ham. "Umm...I'm improving already, don't you think?"

"Yes, dear. Could you pass the salt?"

"Salt?" Eyes wary, she gave him the shaker and watched him generously salt the potatoes. "You don't like my potatoes?"

Justin looked surprised. "Of course I do. They're great! But they need salt."

"Well, you certainly eat enough of them for them to be good!" she cried hotly.

"Kelly, look..." He picked up her hand but she snatched it away. "I used to salt Mom's food, too."

"There you go, comparing me with your mother again!"

He sighed, exasperated. "If a guy can't even salt the potatoes..."

Suddenly she looked at him, awareness stealing over her. "Oh, Justin, what a silly thing to quarrel about."

"I agree—now can I eat my potatoes?"

She nodded, feeling foolish. "I guess I've got a lot to learn—and not just about cooking."

"Like I said, these are great..." he mumbled. And she smiled again.

MORAL: If at dinner you get hot, you may inherit a cold meal.

CLOSING THOUGHTS

1. From the very beginning, you and your husband must work at making a Christian home.
2. There are several things the wife can do to help keep the marriage happy: do them!
3. God is the indispensable third ingredient in a good marriage. Without Him, your home can never be complete.

THOUGHTS FOR YOU

1. QUESTIONS
   A. You have heard the expression, "Their honeymoon is over!" Why would this happen to a marriage? Is it good or bad?

   B. Describe the relationship of the happiest married couple you know. What seems to be the secret of their success?

   C. Ask several married Christian women for some hints on keeping a husband happy. List them below.

2. SCRIPTURES
   Christian attitudes helpful in marriage.
   Galatians 5:22-23
   Ephesians 4:31-32
   1 Corinthians 13:4-5
   James 3:17

Lesson 13

Evaluation and Problem Solving

PROBLEM SOLVING

The following problems are typical of the teen-age years. Based on what you have learned through the study of your previous twelve lessons, you should be able to give sound advice to help solve these problems. Be sure to get to the root—discover the true problem, not just the symptom or result of it. Then write a paragraph or more telling how you could help solve the problem or problems of each girl below. Discuss the problems and your suggestions in class.

CASE #1

Susan had the problem of a bad temper. Even seemingly unimportant things made her angry in a flash. "You must learn to control your temper!" her mother had continually admonished. But until now nothing terrible had happened as a result of her anger.

However, yesterday in physical education class, the girls had been playing volleyball. One of her team mates, a good friend of hers, made a mistake, and Susan hotly "told her off." This made her friend cry and the game broke up. Now her friend won't speak to her and the entire team thinks Susan was a pretty bad character. What should Susan do? How would you recommend for her to avoid future incidents resulting from her bad temper?

CASE #2

Lynda walked home, dejected. Tomorrow night was the night of the annual school banquet and she had no date. Added to that, club elections had been held that day and she also lost out in the two positions for which she'd been nominated. The basketball game was tonight, too, and most of her classmates were either on the team, or were cheerleaders, or had dates for the game. She wasn't going. Somehow she felt totally friendless. What do you suggest for Lynda?

CASE #3

"My parents think I'm a baby!" cried Tina to her best friend. "Everywhere I go, they set a time limit on when I must be in. They have to know where I am, whom I'm with...and I get the third degree when I come home! When am I going to get some freedom? None of my friends' parents treat them this way." Can you suggest some things to help Tina with her problems?

CASE #4

Kristin stared at her report card. Another "D" in English! Besides having difficulty with the subject, she and Miss Farrar just didn't get along well at all. This made it hard for Kristin to ask questions and feel at ease in class. When she approached Miss Farrar about her grade, the teacher had been very busy.

"I can't spend time discussing this with you now, Kristin! But you knew all along what your grades were. If you want to learn, you should stop whispering during class and listen to the lectures!"

Kristin had left, feeling worse than ever. She had been whispering in class only to try to understand the lesson. Miss Farrar never understood her! What should Kristin do to improve both her grades and her relationship with her teacher?

CASE #5

Karen studied her face in the mirror. "Face it, kid," she told herself, "you just don't have what it takes." Her plain square face with its sprinkling of freckles made her frown. "And why couldn't my eyes be a definite color instead of looking like muddy water?"

Tonight most of her girlfriends had dates, but she, as usual, sat home alone. "I'm so ugly," she said aloud, "that nobody will ever date me."

Can you help Karen with her problems?

CASE #6

Church work didn't appeal to Cathy. Despite her parents' teachings and example, she found the Christian life somewhat dull and uneventful. It was much more exciting to be with her school friends than to listen to some Sunday School teacher drone on about the Bible. Sometimes her conscience hurt her a bit for not being more religious, but still she found herself unwilling to try to be a Christian.

What is Cathy's real problem? Can you help her?

CASE #7

Heather and Mark were in love and wanted to be married. Complications, however, continually beset them. "You're too young!" cried Heather's mother. "Eighteen years old and wanting to marry!"

Mark had a good job until May when he received his draft notice from the armed service. Now if he and Heather married, there was sure to be a period of separation without a guarantee that she could join him in his assignment later on.

Heather had a good secretarial position where she had begun work two months ago. She was sure she could support herself, living in a small apartment she and Mark could rent. Her dilemma now is—should she and Mark go ahead and marry?

What advice do you have for Heather?

SELF-EVALUATION

Answer all questions truthfully, just to let yourself know how you've done. Discuss questions 3 and 4 in class if you wish.

1. Have I carefully read each lesson, answered the questions, and studied all scriptures? _____
2. Have I truly made an effort to incorporate the lessons into my life? _____
3. Which lesson dealt with the problem that bothered me most?
   _____
   Did it help me? _____
   Exactly how? _____
4. Which scripture helped and inspired me most? Quote it below.
   _____